6552

There is one who makes himself rich,
yet has nothing;
And one who makes himself poor,
yet has great riches.

Proverbs 13:7

CONSUMED BY SUCCESS

Reaching the top and finding God wasn't there...

REVISED & EXPANDED

ATHENA DEAN

WinePress *Publishing*
Mukilteo, WA 98275

DEDICATION

I dedicate this book to my husband Chuck.
Thanks for standing by me through all my dis-
obedience, and for never giving up on me.
God sure knew what He was doing
when He gave me you.
I love you.

ACKNOWLEDGMENTS

Special thanks go to my children, Aaron, Garrett, Ailen and Roby, for putting up with a mother who was consumed for so many years. I know I've said it before, but I'm sorry. Please forgive me. I love you guys!

Much appreciation also goes to Inger Logelin for her diligence and commitment in the original and second edition editing process. And to Jon Denham of Denham Design, who worked tirelessly on the new cover. Thanks — I could never have done it without you both!

And finally, thank you to all those on-line and across the country who shared their stories with me. While many of them were heartbreaking, they dramatically illustrate a problem we can no longer ignore.

CONTENTS

SECTION III

"Go Forth and Make Money"

SECTION IV

"Setting the Captives Free"

PROLOGUE

When I sensed the Lord telling me that He was giving me a "hard word" for the Body of Christ, I wanted to do a Jonah — run. I had spent the last three years in disobedience, going in a direction opposite to what God had planned for my life. The last thing I wanted to do was revisit that place of rebellion. I needed to obey and share the insights God was giving me.

I make some pretty strong statements in this book. I know I'll be stepping on some toes — because I've been there. I've been sold on the free enterprise system, and the concept of creating financial independence in this lifetime. The system of building a business by selling or consuming products, and recruiting others to do the same was for many years very dear to my heart. I turned a deaf ear to anyone with negative input or attitudes. I was trained to shut out anyone and anything that did not agree with my "success mentality." Those who were not "with us" were the enemy.

Yes, I've been where you, or someone you love, might be at this very moment. I was sold — lock, stock, and barrel — on the pursuit of the American Dream. With blinders on, I continued down a path that almost led to my spiritual destruction.

I hope my story speaks to your heart. You may not agree with my final conclusion, but I trust you'll see that my heart is to see the Body of Christ hungering and thirsting for more of Jesus, rather than success and the things of this world.

I praise God that even when we make a mess of our lives, and finally come to the end of ourselves, He is faithful to forgive us, heal us and deliver us.

Athena Dean

P.S. All names used in this book except for Chuck's and our childrens' are fictional. The stories, however, are true.

SECTION I

"Doing It My Way"

ONE

It's Not What You Have, It's What Has You

The envelope with its blue and gold lettering was in my hand. With my heart pounding in anticipation, I waved it at my husband Chuck.

"How much do you think it is this month?" I asked.

He gazed up into the air as if sighting an object far out of reach. "Hmmm...I'll bet it's $18,000!"

As I pulled it slowly out of the envelope, I saw the numbers spill across the check. My payment for the month was $21,000.00. Not for a year, but for a month!

Chuck playfully snatched the check out of my hand, "Gimme that! I'll make a copy and keep it with the others. Hey, this really proves the dream is real!"

Now, I thought as I looked around me contentedly, *we have enough to live the good life and share with others. We are finally cashing in on all our hard work!*

Our entire family of six was going on a week-long cruise to the Caribbean. Choosing a glitzy resort wardrobe made me feel like a movie star. We were now able to buy the kids the clothes they wanted, and extras like snowboards and skateboards for our teenage sons. Almost completely out of debt, we had just moved into a 3,500-square-foot house with a 180-degree view of Puget Sound. For the first time in many years we had all new furniture in a brand-new house. A shiny mahogany dining room table, beveled glass in the matching china cabinet, a plush oriental rug and elegant maroon and green striped sofas gave the upstairs an exquisite feel. Floor to ceiling windows framed spectacular sunsets, snowy sharp mountain peaks and the ever-changing gray to blue waters of the inland sea. The downstairs rec room where the kids could have their friends over to "hang out" was dominated by a luxury pool table with comfortable couches. It all felt so good.

But, I was consumed! Eaten alive and I didn't even know it! Just that morning I had read in Mark 8, "*What shall it profit a man if he shall gain the whole world and lose his own soul?*" My eyes may have registered the words on the page, but they had not made it to my heart. For months my religious routine had been on automatic pilot — a quick prayer and a few minutes glancing at a Psalm. I couldn't remember the last time I heard God's voice, leading me to a deeper walk with Him.

This financial dream-come-true had its beginnings a few months after Chuck and I were married in 1982. Only five months before, we had been introduced to each other by my roommate, Pat, a mutual friend. At the time, I was managing a successful fund-raising business, and Chuck was selling services for the Church of Scientology. I thought he was a good-looking cowboy with a sense of humor and creativity that intrigued me. He tells me I was so different from any other woman he had ever dated that his curiosity kept him coming back.

He would go shopping with me in my new BMW. I guess he had never seen a woman shop for clothes the way I did. I ripped and tore through long racks of the finest dresses at Bonwit Teller in Beverly Hills. With a flick of my well-used credit card I'd walk out with a pile of expensive dresses and suits. It seemed to Chuck like I had bought half the store. He followed me in amazement. It was a world he had never known, but he didn't plan to leave unless I asked him to. He was having too much fun just watching!

A month after meeting, our friendship went deeper. Chuck had left his camera at my house the night before and returned to pick it up. When I answered the door, we both looked deep into each other's eyes and knew in that instant that for the rest of our lives we would never love anyone else the way we loved each other. I became Mrs. Charles Dean on Valentine's Day — barely two months after we'd met. I was never one to take the slow and steady road whether in shopping or marriage.

Not long after the wedding, Chuck's friend, Jason, invited us to a meeting in Burbank, California. He said he wanted our opinion on a new business venture he was getting into.

"You know, I admire your success in business," he said in his sincerest tone, "and I would like to get your opinion on something. It would really help me out."

That got my attention. He was asking for our opinion! We both felt important and flattered. Of course we could help him out!

"Sure Jason, what can we do to help?"

"Well, you know the construction business here in Southern California is really hurting. I just have to make a change if I'm going to be able to keep up with my house payments and the lease on our two cars. I'm considering going into a new business, and I would like you to come along and check it out. I'd like to see what you think of it; your opinion will help me make my decision whether to get involved or not."

When we walked into the darkened room, a video of an old Phil Donahue show was playing. Donahue was exposing corrupt practices in the insurance industry, the same industry that this new business was going up against. After the video was over, a down-to-earth man in his 40s got up and very eloquently embellished the crusade. He spoke of the common-sense ideas that would help people make and save money, and sound financial principles that had been hidden from the average American family by the greedy insurance and banking industries. The "wrong" that was being perpetrated on innocent consumers quickly began to draw us in.

The speaker then began to paint the picture of the deception of the corporate dream.

"Do you really think your company is going to be there for you when you retire? Do you really think that corporation cares about you and your family?"

He was weaving a feeling of discontentment for working nine to five for a paycheck and benefits from a big corporation who wouldn't be there for you when you really needed them.

"What would you do with an extra $1,000 or $1,500 a month? Buy a new house, car, RV? Send your kids to private school? Travel? Retire early?" the speaker questioned. Our minds were reeling with possibilities and stirrings of dissatisfaction and greed.

Next he began to explain the incredible compensation plan. "You could start your business and make an extra $500, $1,000, or $2,000 a month — part time!" If we followed certain steps of sales, and recruited friends and family, our income would increase accordingly. The clincher came when he introduced a 26-year-old guy who was making $25,000 a month after only 18 months in the business! This really did it for us. If he could do it, so could we! When he said he only had 20 kits for people to buy to get started, we scrambled to the front of the room to claim ours!

At the time, our fund-raising business, in which Chuck was helping me, felt like a ball and chain around our necks. This opportunity seemed like something that could really give us some financial independence. We could spend time working hard to build the business, but then we would be able to do what we pleased while it continued to generate income. It felt as though we were getting in on the California Gold Rush — and we wanted to sink our picks and shovels into it before anyone else!

What we were sinking our lives into was network (or multi-level) marketing.

We rushed home and began to share the "dream" with our four young children. It could be the answer to all their dreams; the thing that allowed us to have all the toys we'd ever wanted! Chuck's daughter and son from a previous marriage, Roby and Ailen, were eleven and seven years old. They were definitely old enough to grasp what money could buy. They started dreaming of closets full of new clothes and bicycles and toys of every description. And even though Garrett and Aaron, my two and three year old boys, were too young to understand what was happening, they got excited with the rest of us.

We were so enthralled with the opportunity that it didn't dawn on us that our friend Jason wasn't just thinking about joining the company. He wasn't really looking for our opinion. All along his plan was to recruit us. We were on his "hot list" and the "opinion line" that he used was the one he thought would get us to a meeting. That line worked on us, so we in turn used the same technique on the prospects we eventually listed out.

The California "Gold Rush"

As we sat down eagerly with our "upline manager" we were told to make a list of at least 100 people, everyone from our friends and family to the clerk at the local grocery store and the pastor at church.

"Think of every possible person you can, and just write their names down on a piece of paper," said our manager. He even gave us a memory jogger so we wouldn't miss anyone. As we read the words, "school, church, PTA, relatives, the clerk at the grocery store, the person who sold you your last car," my mind began to churn with long lists of names.

"When you finish listing everyone, go back and put a star next to the people who are in some form of leadership; people who have a following, people who are excited, motivated, hard-working, successful; people who influence others. These are the ones we want to recruit into your organization because they are the kind of people that others will follow."

They didn't exactly say it, but they wanted to use our relationships, our credibility with people and our resources to get their business in front of qualified prospects and make sales and recruit more people, starting the process of 100 names all over again.

Chuck and I are nothing if not outgoing, so we made up a list of 200 prospects and threw a big party at our house so we would have a captive audience for our very first opportunity meeting. We invited everyone we knew to hear the good news! The barbecue was smoking out in the back yard, and festive music was playing in the background. Jason and his upline managers were there to help us "work the crowd."

We were totally convinced that we were helping our friends. After all, we had a great product. It would make and save them money. Why, it could save their lives! Our zeal to help ourselves by helping others was born. After dessert, we gathered everyone around a white board and our upline manager began to share the dream.

The fund-raising business I had established a few years earlier helped raise needed capital for local non-profit organizations. It was showing signs of weakening, so as fast as we could we shut that down and went full-time into our new crusade. With no second thoughts, we opened an office above a real estate firm in Burbank and ran newspaper ads all over town. We held two opportunity meetings a day and turned into a well-oiled recruiting machine. With each new recruit we'd sit down and help them make that all-important list.

"Let's face it, the people who will want to help you the most are those who love you and care about you! And how could you possibly hesitate to go to those closest to you first? You owe it to your friends and family to share this important information with them! If you're active in a church, that's a great place to start!" We would encourage them with such intensity that they never questioned us or our tactics. We told a very convincing story. After all, we were sold and knew that they should be as well!

As Chuck and I built our business, we had great training from the charismatic and motivational ex-football coach who owned the company.

"We're looking for people who want to make a difference with their lives. If you want to do something special with your life and *be somebody,* this is the place to do it! We need leaders, those with character and strength, with courage and hope. We have an answer to the dilemma of the financial situation so many families find themselves in. This is a time in history like no other. You have a chance to change the financial future of your family and the generations to follow. You have a chance to change others lives as well as your own. You can't afford to let this opportunity pass you by. So just do it! Don't make excuses, just do it! Don't whine and complain about your situation, just do it! Don't listen to others who tell you that you can't make it, just do it!"

Being new to multi-level marketing ourselves, we were total sponges and modeled ourselves after the most successful of all the leaders in the company. And we always knew who was the most successful. Every month a list of the top earners came out and everyone's cash-flow was listed from top to bottom. There weren't many women on that list, so that really motivated me!

Our leader really knew how to get us to produce. At regional and national rallies, he would give out T-shirts that said "I Am Somebody" or some other trite statement that made us feel important and recognized. Those T-shirts really got our competitive juices flowing. Some people would do *anything* (including work 18 hours a day, seven days a week) just to have their names called to go up and get a Tshirt. As I look back I realize those rooms were filled with incredibly needy people who lived and breathed for this "father figure" to tell them they amounted to something! And I was one of those people.

We would frequently hear what it would take to make it big. Of course, making it big always translated into having a big house, new car, and a $100,000+ annual income.

Chuck and I would frequently parrot the words back to each other of what it would take to win.

"It's going to take incredible sacrifice, total commitment, a will to win, hard work, long hours, intensity and endurance. Not just for a week or a month, but however long it takes to win!"

"Yes," we'd say to each other, "and we'll just do it!"

The challenge filled us with a sense of noble purpose. How much better could it get? A chance to make big, big money and help people at the same time. This was a crusade, to right the wrongs of American big business. We were the good guys, the white hats, the knights in shining armor.

We worked night and day at a feverish pitch that first year. Ailen was involved in Little League and Roby was active in drama in school. While they searched the audiences to find our faces at games and plays, they never did spot us. We were too busy chasing the dream to make time to attend their activities. Those kids hardly ever saw us, but they saw plenty of the baby sitters. We rushed them from school to day care to baby sitters to home, shuffling them from one person's care to the other. We held the idea close that it would eventually be worth the sacrifice. I only wish the kids felt the same way.

"Mom, why don't we ever get to see you anymore?" Garrett would ask.

"Oh, honey, it won't be like this forever. Just a little while and we'll be able to spend lots more time with you guys!" I was so intense about making it big that I wasn't very sensitive to the pain in his voice. He kept asking hard questions like that, but I kept giving the same pat answer. We promised ourselves and them that it wouldn't last for long. We planned to build the business to the point where the momentum would self-propel and then we could kick back and have that quality time with our kids that we were sacrificing on a daily basis. We weren't the only ones believing the lie that if we just work a few more hours now, later we could make it up to our kids and spouse by having financial freedom. For many others that day never came, and we saw families deteriorate and become destroyed one by one.

Marina, a Mexican-American with a fiery personality, was a real leader. She moved up the ladder in our company quickly, while her husband groped to find meaningful employment. Since she was so busy building her business, he took over the role of mothering their two-year-old son and three-year-old daughter. The more recognition and honor she received from her peers and the "boss," the less respect she had for her struggling husband. It wasn't long before they separated and then divorced. She continued to pursue success in the company, but lost custody of her kids as her husband took them to live with his parents. The last time I saw her she was experiencing a measure of success, but the hollow look in her eyes told another story.

Brian and Mary had spent years building their business without ever really getting anywhere. People around them found success, but it always seemed to elude their grasp. Brian spent so much time trying to "make it big" that they became two strangers in the same house. Mary became bitter and resentful toward her husband because so many other men were more successful. He just couldn't seem to measure up and this began to be the source of many heated arguments. Breaking their seven-year-old son's heart, they separated and were divorced. Both these couples were professing Christians. Their Christian lives seemed to go on auto-pilot as they walked in complete disobedience to God's Word.

Being Somebody

At the regional awards event of our financial services multi-level, Chuck looked handsome and successful in his black tuxedo. I sat next to him in my new pink, backless silk dress with my heart pounding in anticipation of hearing my name called out over the sound system. I was pretty sure we had done enough to qualify for the big promotion to regional vice-president, but you never really knew until they called you up on stage. Everyone seemed to be living for this moment. The title meant you were now in business for yourself and had the opportunity to *be somebody*.

"Chuck and Athena Dean." I smiled triumphantly as I heard the applause start. We had made it to that esteemed regional vice-presidential position in just 12 months. No one had done it as quickly as we had. This made me feel especially important and satisfied. We were well on our way to riches.

One year after our marriage to each other and to multi-level marketing, we made the decision to move to the Northwest, to Washington where Chuck had grown up. He then began to lose interest in the business once we had opened up the office in Washington. I think he began to see that I seemed to love the business more than I loved him, and he was jealous. The more he distanced himself from the business, the more I lost interest in him. It seemed that I was married to my work and he was now taking on the neglected spouse syndrome. Depressed and always complaining, his communication was mostly critical and nagging. Whenever I would come home, Chuck would whine about the kids, the housework, about being stressed out. Perhaps he thought by getting me out of California, life would slow down a little and I would have more time for him.

"All you care about is that damn business. You never have any time for me or the kids. We don't even know you anymore. You spend all your time pleasing your clients and your downline, but we don't even rate the time of day."

At times he was like a jealous lover, being very suspicious about everything that I did. "So, where were you tonight? Did it really have to take this long for you to finish your training appointment? Why is it that I get the feeling that you'd rather be out working than home with us?"

It got to the point where I did anything I could just to stay away from home so I wouldn't have to hear his complaining. Almost every six months we seemed on the brink of divorce, but somehow managed to stay together. Each time I would give him an ultimatum. "Either you accept me the way I am, or I am leaving."

He would then stifle his dissatisfaction with the way our marriage was going and we would stay together. My workaholism and drive for recognition was now in full force and Chuck simply decided to put up with it just to keep our marriage together.

The truth was not as good as the dream. Even though by this time we were cash-flowing $50,000 a year, our overhead was so high that we were perpetually broke. I would always have expensive office rent, huge long distance bills, advertising bills that never seemed to end, and a travel and entertainment tab that was sky high. I never operated on a budget, I just spent and spent and spent, and somehow always generated enough cash to just keep up with the payments. Even when we hit the coveted $100,000 mark, our expenses far exceeded our income. The need to look successful until it actually happened resulted in huge lease payments on cars, offices, furniture, and our home. While everything on the outside looked great and our numbers on the leader sheets were always at the top, our marriage was on the edge of disaster and the stress of our financial situation only added fuel to the fire.

I was held captive — a prisoner of my own grasping and lustful heart. While I thought I was proving my success by the things I had, those things actually had me. I was miserable. Since I had never learned to value relationships, my dreams for my marriage, family and personal life revolved only around having things, not about anything of lasting value.

TWO

Looking for Love in All the Wrong Places

I've been told I'm a capable person, someone who gets things accomplished. Through experience I've found that God has gifted me with the ability to organize, inspire and lead large groups of people toward a stated goal. Part of my gift-mix is the ability to learn quickly any new technique or lesson. Picking up on things and doing them well right off the bat isn't hard for me. My weak points center around my inability to get close to people, as well as allow them to get close to me. Because of this weakness, I can put more importance on projects than on people, with more desire for business than for relationships. I also tend to be very self-centered. It's a real struggle to think of the needs of other people before I think about myself. Good relationships don't just come naturally for me. One unsavory trait that stems from my selfishness is my sloppiness around the house. I guess I'm a messie, and Chuck is definitely a cleanie. My side of the bed is always like a minefield; I can let it pile up for days before Chuck's discomfort motivates me to clean up my mess.

I'm like my father in my shortcomings as well as my ability to sell. He was a workaholic who put his entire life into success and the things it afforded him, never giving much time and effort to the relationships he had with those who loved him the most.

Like my dad, I'm also an excitable person and smile a lot. If I like something, I say so, and others get excited in the process. There's certainly nothing wrong with the positive gifts God gave me, as long as they don't get used in the wrong way. For a long time, I believed that business was where I was supposed to use my abilities, even after I had my heart changed by God!

A Longing for God

I remember recognizing that I had a longing for God when I was around nine years old. Whenever we visited my cousins in Alabama, we would go with them to the Catholic church. Walking into the towering church building, I felt a quiet reverence for God that I had never experienced before. It felt like there was something holy there, that the awesomeness of the God of the universe was resident in that place. It was a new experience for me to be in a place where people desired to surrender their lives to God. I had never been exposed to spiritual things or church attendance at home. I can remember wanting what I felt God had for me. One time I thought about what it would be like to become a nun.

Even at that young time in my life, I was pretty wild and boy crazy, so that idea didn't last for long! When we would go visit my aunt and uncle, I always got my cousin, Kerrie, in trouble. I wanted to meet all the boys in the neighborhood, so we would sit out on the balcony, playing our Sonny and Cher music at full blast trying to get some attention. Unfortunately, the only attention we got was from Uncle Henry and his leather belt. My longing for spiritual things was quickly replaced with trying to get attention from boys.

I was also falling in love with horses and the equestrian world. The chance to compete in horse shows, to be the only one on a horse in the middle of the ring competing for the blue ribbon or championship, intrigued me. This was something I could pour my life into. This, too, became an all-consuming passion for me. Soon I had dreams of being the best and competing in all the big-time horse shows.

"Look at Me!"

"See, Dad! I can do it! Look at me!"

My entire childhood was spent trying to get my dad to notice me. When he would compliment me and tell me things about myself that would lift me up and make me feel special, I would feel fulfilled and complete. I would feel whole and loved. The words that he spoke to me in my childhood have had an impact on me that influenced me as an adult. This influence has not always been positive.

I didn't have a problem getting my mom to take note of all I did. She came to every horse show and every practice session. She was such a perfectionist that she wanted me to do everything exactly right.

"Athena, keep your toes in, and your heels down. Sit up straight! You look like a slouch!"

I know she meant well, but the frequent criticism communicated rejection to my young heart. It never seemed to fail that mother would let me know that I didn't measure up to my "perfect" big brother. Jim was quiet and cooperative, never giving my mother any flak. He was an A student and liked all the things she did — classical music, opera, and intellectual things. I was a strong-willed child to the extreme, always pushing my mother to the limits of her patience. I never dressed the way she liked, nor followed the rules of etiquette at the dinner table that she expected. I always wanted my own way.

My dad, on the other hand, was very nurturing. He would sing songs to me from old commercials, and tell me stories about myself.

"Athena, if there was a field of a thousand little girls in it, and if I was flying over in my helicopter, I would look over the other 999 little girls and pick **you** out, because you are so special. You know why you are special? Because you are **you**!"

He recognized me and made me feel important. But because he was such a workaholic, those times of nurturing were few and far between.

He started out knocking on doors to sell encyclopedias, and ended up the executive vice-president of sales for Encyclopedia Britannica. With this climb up the ladder came a lot of travel and a great passion for success and wealth. My mom raised us and my dad made sure that we had everything we wanted. At one point I had five horses and was showing four of them every weekend in horse shows. This was a very expensive hobby, but it was something that I loved to do, so my parents were 100 percent behind me. We lived in a house with an indoor swimming pool in one of the most affluent suburbs of Chicago. My dad would land his helicopter on the hockey field of the private school I attended in Wisconsin, and fly me down to ride my horses on the weekends.

I got along pretty well with my peers, but I always had to out-do them, which I'm sure got old for them after a while. I always tried to win — and usually did — in the games we'd play. I had to make sure everyone knew I was the best!

I know my dad believed that giving me the opportunity to succeed in competitive riding was important. Once my mom lectured me on what a sacrifice it was for my dad to spend so much money on me so that I could have the chance to compete in all the horse shows.

I knew these opportunities were not available to every other girl my age, but still felt empty. Looking back I can see that I would rather have had time and relationship instead of privileges and things. I wondered, *if I wasn't a winner, would dad still love me?* This question haunted me.

I felt I had to compete for his attention by always winning the blue ribbon, and did so with a drive that seemed insatiable. I would compete in every horse show I could, getting there early in the morning to be the first one at the barn, practicing after school every day. I was consumed with being the best in my class.

One time when my dad was in town for a horse show, I finished a round with a perfect score. I looked out into the audience to see him with a "thumbs up" gesture and a big smile on his face. That simple acknowledgment made my insides feel warm and my life seem complete. Yet the fear of being rejected by my dad still burned deep within me. It fueled the competitive thrust that would be a dominant factor in my actions and decisions of the rest of my life.

The combination of my energetic, driven personality and my craving for love and recognition took me down a road where I would find myself consumed by finding the horse of my dreams, the man of my dreams, and the business of my dreams. In my first marriage, I found that relationships could be dangerous, but that I could hide myself in my work. Since that relationship failed, I began a quest for a business that would fulfill all the desires of my heart. When, at 33 years of age, I asked Jesus to be my Savior, the void began to be filled. But even then I continued to be unconsciously consumed by the need to be important.

Trying Hard Not to Get Saved!

Chuck and I had been married for four years when Jesus finally got a hold of my heart. I was making big money in insurance and securities, and month in and month out ranked in the top two percent of the company. On paper I was successful, but my personal life was falling apart.

When Chuck and I married, I had no idea that he was a Vietnam veteran and what significance that would have on our relationship. Every time we went to a party where there was alcohol and drugs, he would overdo it. He drank and partied with a crazy flair to which I couldn't relate. His wild, drunken streaks and loud, boisterous fun were not fun to me. In his drunken states, he tried to communicate some deep emotional thoughts to me, but I didn't really care to hear it.

I became alarmed when Chuck got involved in an organization that protested paying taxes and radically opposed the current government structure of the United States. This "patriot" movement really hit a chord with Chuck, and he soon became a fanatic. I, who rarely like to rock the boat, found myself married to a man who was on the verge of personal disaster. He felt he needed to change the government, the tax system, the license system, and every other system connected with modern American life. In a period of three months, he had submitted affidavits to three branches of the government, revoking his driver's license, social security number, marriage license, and fishing license. He sent them all back and declared himself a natural-born citizen of the United States who did not need to be licensed to be a citizen. He returned his license plate to the secretary of state and mounted his own plate, which read, "Just Skip It."

During the course of a year, I threatened several times to kick Chuck out. When the IRS and state's attorney general came to visit, I was scared and furious. The authorities started coming after Chuck for his questionable practices of using a "warehouse bank" to turn his federal reserve notes into gold and silver without reporting it to the IRS. My business was threatened and I was ready to call it quits with the marriage.

Chuck's convictions were strong. He'd rant, "I don't see how you can sell people those so-called investments when they aren't even backed by real money! Those IRAs are just 'air money' as far as I'm concerned!"

"As if you're going to change the entire government by turning in your license plates!" I'd counter. "Get real, Chuck! You can't just drop out of the system!"

We were on opposite sides of the philosophical spectrum and there was no middle ground. Business was my life, and without realizing it, I had put my husband and children down at the bottom of my priority list. I was so self-centered and consumed with getting what I wanted, that I couldn't even see that my husband was crying out for help. I just wasn't listening.

I had made up my mind. The relationship was over. Here I was planning to end my marriage and still thinking I was a success because I was making over $100,000 a year! Oh, how deceived I was! I spent the weekend away at a business retreat. About 40 of the people in my downline gathered at a Christian retreat center up in the mountains and spent the weekend sharing our dreams, bonding, goal setting and encouraging one another.

When I returned home, I found a person I did not recognize. Yes, it was Chuck, but he was different somehow. *He seems so peaceful...I wonder what has gotten into him?* I watched his face as he spoke to me and his countenance was lighter. He was no longer crying and groveling around feeling sorry for himself. I couldn't put my finger on it, but I noticed that I was not as anxious for him to leave. He had a peace about him that was unexplainable. When I had left for the weekend, he was a sniveling wreck. He would cry at the drop of a hat and try to get me to change my mind about divorcing him. Now he was serene and calm. What had happened? This was not the Chuck Dean I was used to.

A few hours later, one of my business associates told me that Chuck had accepted Jesus into his heart as Lord and Savior. I was stunned. Chuck, a Christian? No way! That was against everything we ever stood for and believed in! We thought Christians were wimps. After all, when you're as talented and able as we were, who needs a crutch like Jesus?

We had been in and out of Scientology, The Church Universal Triumphant, meditation, astrology, channeling —

and now Christianity? Our involvement in the new age felt very safe. Each so-called religion we got involved with believed that man was basically good and that we could determine our own destiny. These beliefs had helped me to become more and more hardened to the gospel as they communicated that only weaklings needed Jesus. With Chuck getting saved, I felt we were going backwards. But I didn't let it bother me too much, because I was still divorcing him.

Three days later, the Lord had softened my heart to the point that I heard myself saying, "Well, I guess you don't have to go."

"Oh, Athena, I can't believe this! I knew God would heal our marriage! Thank you, Jesus!"

This was a totally new Chuck. Now I had a dilemma. If we were going to stay together and Chuck was going to be one of those Christians, then I would probably need to be one too, just so we'd have something in common. I worried about telling all the people who knew what wimps I thought Christians were that now I was one! This was very difficult for me. I knew I needed to be saved, but my pride was getting the best of me. My heart continued to be softened because of the incredible changes I continued to witness in my husband. He was soft, tender, loving and gentle, yet he was strong, confident and courageous. I tried hard **not** to get saved, because I didn't want to be seen as weak.

Five weeks after Chuck got saved, my upline in the financial services business, also a Christian, was in town. "Monty, I know I need to say this prayer to make sure I am saved. Would you help me through it? I just don't know exactly what to do." I asked if he would lead me in the sinner's prayer. As I prayed, I felt overwhelming relief in knowing I'd been forgiven for all the rebellion and sin in my life. The thing I'd resisted for so long was finally part of my life. I felt like a new person — washed clean for the first time in my life. The load of guilt that had weighed me down and made me unhappy and hard, was gone for good. I felt like my heart of stone had been replaced with a heart of flesh.

My Kingdom Come!

I had no foundation or understanding of the Word of God; it just wasn't a part of my upbringing. On the other hand, Chuck, whose father was a pastor, had a huge amount of biblical knowledge imbedded into his mind as a child and it all came flooding back to him. He understood the elements of faith and the importance of renewing his mind with the Word of God. We were worlds apart even after we were both saved. Chuck had surrendered completely to Jesus, but I was standing firm in my pride.

Somehow, deep down, I knew that if I really surrendered to Jesus, He would ask me to give up my drive for wealth and recognition. I just wasn't ready for that. I wanted *my* kingdom to come and *my* will to be done. I might have been on my way to heaven, but the last thing I wanted to leave behind was my world of competition, success and recognition. I struggled with the guilt that I felt over the fact that I didn't really want the Lord to come soon. There was an enmity in my soul and the flesh seemed to be winning out, because as I prayed and went to church, I still longed for the things of this world.

The people I was involved with in my business had become my family. They made me feel good, and I wasn't about to give that up for anyone, not even the Lord. My business family gave me the strokes that made me feel good about myself. They never asked me "hard" questions about how my relationships with my children were going or what my real motives were for working so hard. I was putting in about 70 hours a week and any social life I enjoyed was centered around my business. If a person didn't help build my business, I didn't waste my time building a relationship with him or her. It wasn't something I consciously thought about, but I had been brainwashed into believing that I should pour my life into those who would be successful, because their success would bring me success. The truth is that, since my children didn't make me any money and didn't help build my business, even my time with them was at an absolute minimum. It was easier for me to stay away from them so that I wouldn't have to confront the pain I had caused them. If I wasn't around, I wouldn't have to hear the haunting questions and comments they would inevitably make.

"When will you be home? You're never home."

While Chuck and I now had Jesus in common, we were still married singles with completely different missions in life. I spent my every waking hour thinking about the business and how I could make it better. All he cared about after getting saved was telling others about the Lord. He wanted to see millions come to Jesus. I still wanted to make my millions. One day Chuck came home from Bible school where he had been reading a book by Oswald Chambers called *So Send I You* and said, "We're going!"

"We're going are we? And where to, pray tell?" I answered.

"To Africa, Asia, Russia, I don't care. I just know that we're supposed to go!" Chuck answered with such intensity it almost knocked me over.

I responded sourly, "Great dear, I hope you have a good time!"

I had accepted Jesus as my Savior, but *I* was still the lord of my life.

THREE

It All Sounded So Good!

By spending 70 hours a week on becoming an expert in my financial services business, I felt I was on my way to what I called success. Eventually I became an expert on network marketing and even wrote books about how to succeed in that arena. I was on fire. I would wake up at 6:00 A.M. with my wheels turning. A rush of adrenaline would surge through me as I anticipated what the day would hold. It seemed I never got tired or lacked energy. From that first early morning cup of coffee to the last satisfied look at my daytimer in the evening, I was completely focused and intense. My business was my life. If people or things didn't relate somehow to my business, I wasn't interested.

I didn't know much about multi-level marketing when I first started. I just wanted the business to help me achieve my goals. My main goal was to create financial independence — to have that nice house, drive a BMW or Mercedes, to have the good life where money would never be an issue. I thought I would then be free from having to answer to anyone. I would be able to do as I pleased.

As I learned the inner workings of multi-level marketing (or MLM for short), I could identify with its common
sense way of doing business. I learned that it combines two
proven ideas in the world of business: networking and marketing. Marketing is the business practice of moving goods
and services through distribution channels, from the manufacturer to the consumer. Networking is the joining of
people who share resources and knowledge to accomplish
common goals. In a MLM business, you develop a network
of people by recruiting them into your organization, also
called a downline. Through that network of people, the
company's products or services are sold. Sometimes, the
distributor is the consumer. Or the distributor sells the product or service to the consumer. Either way, without the distributor buying for personal use or selling to make a profit,
the company doesn't make any money.

Rather than spending a predetermined amount on advertising, the company pays the distributor to advertise their
product by word of mouth. Distributors make their money
from personal sales, bonuses, and override commissions on
the sales volume of the distributors in their downline. The
network is created by recruiting and selling to friends, relatives, neighbors and acquaintances.

Multi-level marketing has many names, such as network marketing, direct selling, direct marketing, direct sales
and the like. Most companies have figured out that multi-
level marketing has developed a bad reputation, so they go
to great lengths to try to make their distribution system
sound like something else.

One lady I met recently was involved in a home party
plan that sold jewelry. She was offended that I would label
her company as multi-level, adamantly insisting that it was

not. She had over 20 people in her organization and was encouraged to build a larger organization so she could make overrides on others and not have to work so hard at it herself.

If you have to recruit distributors in order to make the big money, it's definitely some form of multi-level marketing, no matter what name it is being called.

Cruising for Christians

"Just think, Chuck," I mused out loud, "if I can just make it to senior vice-president, I'll qualify for an extra $10,000 a month! If I could get some other believers involved we could all make our dreams come true for the Lord."

Chuck agreed that there was plenty we could do with that extra money each month. "Just think of all the vets we could get saved," he said, thinking of all the places he could travel to reach them.

It all sounded so good! I would recruit other Christians into my business and make a ton of money so my husband could be supported in full-time ministry!

Shortly after coming to the Lord, Chuck enrolled in Cascade Bible College in Bellevue, Washington, to catch up on all he'd missed. While there he heard about Point Man Ministries, a Christian outreach for Vietnam veterans by Vietnam veterans.

For 17 years Chuck had denied even being a veteran. Once he got saved and the Lord miraculously healed him of his post-traumatic stress symptoms, he began to have a heart to reach other vets. After praying, he felt that Point Man Ministries was where the Lord would want him to serve. When the ministry's founder died suddenly, his widow asked Chuck to take over the ministry. He spent all his time creating a network of Christian Vietnam veterans to help those vets who still hadn't come all the way home (spiritually). He found other born-again Vietnam veterans who had a burden to share their relationships with Jesus with other hopeless and hurting vets.

Looking back, I can see how I had used the good motivation of funding the ministry to justify my lust for more of the world. I convinced myself that I was doing a good thing for people. After all, with a lot of money, I could give to missions and help other Christians get out of debt. But in my heart I was far from seeking God's perfect will for my life.

Who Do You Know?

It became easy for me to use and abuse my relationships in the church to get where I wanted to go. My standard line went something like this: "John, I know how busy you are with your ministry, but who do you know who might be interested in earning an extra $500 to $1,000 a month part time?" Of course, my intention was to recruit John. By using this back door approach I'd learned from another top producer, I found people more open to listening to my pitch. My goal was to find or create relationships with those in the church who had influence with large numbers of people. I would do so by asking for their help. I would find people with followings and then ask if they could help me out by referring me to others who might need what I had. Pastors, their wives, and anyone involved in the ministry were ideal targets. So many people would want to help them, I felt it would be simple for them to build a business.

"Jane, we've got so many other people in the ministry involved," I'd say convincingly. "It has proven to be a great way to fund new projects and help with additional ministry expenses. And it'll be easy for you to build your business fast as there'll be so many people who will want to help you."

I justified my practices with the thoughts of the good I knew I could do with the money. Why, I could fund the printing and distribution of *Reveille*, Point Man's free newspaper for vets. After all, printing and mailing 25,000 - 50,000 copies required money! I could help underwrite the new building project at church, as well as take on a few more foreign missionaries. Denial ruled and greed kicked in. I was blind to the lie I had bought that the end justified the means. Ideas of moving up to a nicer house with a view, trading in my car for a newer, more expensive model, taking the family on a cruise, buying a new wardrobe, and having extra spending money began to crowd out the godly things I planned for the money.

I was so busy working, I never really listened for God's voice. I just did whatever I thought sounded good and then asked God to bless it! Eager to build my business fast, I spent freely on advertising in the newspapers, on the radio, and upgrading offices, all the while operating without a budget. I was addicted to work and liked being in control. I wanted to build a big business for the recognition I would receive more than I wanted to glorify God. I'm ashamed to say that I was more excited about making money than I was about Jesus!

The last thing in the world I wanted to do was obey 1 John 2:15 and 16:

Do not love the world or the things of the world. If anyone loves the world the love of the Father is not in him. For all that is in the world, the lust of the flesh, the lust of the eyes, and the pride of life is not of the Father but is of the world.

I know I was not the only one in deception. There are countless numbers of sincere Christians who have succumbed to this same deception in the American church. In my business, we always taught our new recruits that the church was the best place to go to get recruits.

One man I know created an entire informational meeting to present at churches. His strategy was to attract one or two sharp individuals who he could get excited about the business. Then they would sell and recruit the rest of the church body. Another woman I knew used to go from church to church, getting involved in women's Bible studies and offering to lead praise and worship. In reality, she was just going to meet new people and find more prospects for her business.

I found out that advertising on Christian radio was the ultimate bonanza! This is not to say that Christians are naive, but they just seem to assume that people advertising on Christian radio must be genuinely born-again, or they wouldn't be advertising on there. There are many companies run by Mormons actively advertising on Christian radio! Compared to advertising on secular stations, I found the Christian radio audience to be trusting and even gullible. It was amazingly easy to sell and recruit networks of believers from hundreds of churches across the country simply by running an ad campaign on nationwide Christian radio.

My intention is not to point the finger at multi-level marketing only. Network marketing isn't the only kind of business that uses the Body of Christ to build its ranks. Almost every sales organization I know of that manufactures consumer items encourages its sales people to utilize their personal relationships to build up their business. Whether it's real estate, insurance, automobiles, cosmetics, vitamins, or even a privately-owned retail establishment, those who represent their products or services will usually look for prospects at their place of worship.

Bill started selling real estate a few years ago. He was very well trained and provided a great service to his clients. When he became a Christian, he just automatically networked at church, exchanging business cards with other parishioners before and after church, and "working the crowd" every chance he got. Before long he was listing and selling so many houses he hardly had time to come to church. When he did, it was not to get fed and grow in the things of God, it was to do business.

After much prayer and conviction by the Holy Spirit, I can now see that by bringing business into the church, we have become like the money changers in the temple. Jesus did not take what these men were doing lightly. He said, *"Take these things away! Do not make my father's house a house of merchandise!"* (John 2:16). Oh, how we defile the house of God by bringing our business with us to church!

FOUR

God's Idea or
Good Idea?

I had been saved for 18 months and knew that I could not go on justifying being motivated by money. I knew in my heart I was living an idolatrous life. Money, not Jesus, was my Lord and I had gone too long bowing down and worshipping mammon.

One of the prayers I began to say every day without expecting the Lord to answer was, "Your will, not mine, Lord. Have Your way. Use me, Lord. Change my heart to desire Your will."

I was then making over $100,000 a year and wasn't satisfied. We were actually thinking about moving back to California, because all of the top earners who stayed down there when we moved to Washington were now making twice the income I was.

Chuck was willing to put Point Man on hold to help me build the business one more time, so that it could really fund the ministry the way we wanted. One Sunday evening Chuck had been invited to share his testimony at our church. It was strange but in the year and a half that we had been saved, this was the first time I was going to hear my husband share his testimony. He was the executive director of a growing ministry to veterans, and had led literally hundreds of men to the Lord since he got saved. I had been so busy with "my thing" that I didn't even know what was happening in his life. As I sat in the back row and listened to him share, I wept. I saw his heart and began to see how God was using him.

Just then I felt the Lord speaking quietly to my heart. *Walk away from the business and help Chuck in the ministry.*

It seemed so clearly from the Lord, but fear immediately set in. I decided that the voice I heard deep in my heart was definitely *not* God!

A few minutes later a lady approached me who didn't have a clue about our situation or plans. She said, "Don't be surprised if your plans change." I was stunned. That really was God!

I knew then that the Lord was calling me to leave the business behind and help my husband in ministry. At that point the ministry income was about $500 a month. How was a family of six going to exist on that? But now I knew it was God, so I wasn't worried. God was changing my heart to desire His will, and He was having His way, just as I had prayed.

God's Way of Doing Business

As I began to make the transition and turn my business over to my upline director, I had many thoughts about how I could help build Point Man. I knew there had to be grant money available for an organization that was helping the hurting Vietnam veterans. I planned to build Point Man's donor base by mailing out letters to raise support. As we submitted what I thought were great ideas to the Lord, He made it clear that He had another plan in mind.

Pray. That was all He said.

I thought, *Sure, God, pray! I've got to do something, don't I? No.*

God was wanting to prove to us, especially to me, that He is the provider. If I brought in the money by great fund-raising programs, how would I ever know if it was God or me who was making it all happen? He wanted me to learn to trust Him, and that meant staying out of the way so He could provide in His own way!

There were times when we ate out of the food bank, but God was always faithful.

One Friday morning a disconnect notice arrived for non-payment of the ministry phone bill. If we didn't pay $400 by Monday at 5:00 P.M., they would turn off the phones. I couldn't get an extension, this was the end of the line, and we had no money in the bank. I was worried since most of our donations came through the mail and there was to be no mail on Monday because it was a holiday. We had only one more day in which something could possibly come through the mail.

God had my attention! I was desperate for an answer. I didn't know what to do so I went away for the night to a retreat center where I could fast and pray. I was sure that God was trying to say something to me. Was it some awful sin I'd committed? Had I somehow mishandled the finances of the ministry? Was that why we had a lack of money?

As I began to pray and repent for everything I could possibly think of, God began to show me something totally unrelated to money. He brought to mind my habit of being disrespectful towards my husband. I'd make fun of Chuck, just to get a laugh. My sarcastic attitude was grieving the Holy Spirit, and it took a financial disaster to get my attention! After I repented for wrong attitudes towards my husband, I felt a spiritual release and went home.

Sunday afternoon the doorbell rang. Marc, a Vietnam vet we ministered to occasionally, was at the door. Marc often struggled with unemployment.

"I don't know why," he said, "but the Lord told me to empty out my savings account and give you this money." Marc handed Chuck and me exactly four hundred dollars!

The Lord met our needs over and over again, in many creative ways. It never ceased to amaze us the way He would orchestrate circumstances to help our faith grow. He was always faithful to provide for our family. The next five years were filled with adventures in faith as we followed His lead in the ministry.

Still, there were areas of my heart that I had not completely yielded to the Lord.

Setting a Bad Example

Being a Type-A workaholic personality, I threw myself into ministry work with the same intensity that I put into my business. Soon, the ministry became as much of an idol to me as striving for money and success in business had. I had never slowed down long enough to let the Lord heal areas in my life that were causing the dysfunctional behavior. So, I set an unhealthy and actually damaging example for others in the ministry.

We worked six days a week and sometimes seven for five years without ever taking a break. Sundays we would often speak in churches. Our children were neglected by both of us now, which wasn't much of a witness for Christ. The need in the veteran community was so great that we found ourselves ministering over the phone after work hours. We wanted to always be available to meet the needs of those who were hurting. This schedule took its toll on us and burnout set in. Watchman Nee refers to the "wearing down tactics of Satan." That was happening in our lives. I had allowed people and circumstances to wear me down to the point where I was totally operating in the flesh the last year we were involved in the ministry.

Although I was not where I should have been spiritually, I was beginning to minister powerful truths to women about healing from post-traumatic stress syndrome (PTS) at conferences. We were finding that, just as veterans experienced post-traumatic stress, women who were not veterans often had the same syndrome. Anyone who has experienced trauma or severe wounding in her life is susceptible. The symptoms are depression, rage, isolation, difficulty with close personal relationships, suicidal tendencies, and substance abuse.

When Chuck and I first began ministering to veterans, I thought, *Oh, you poor things, you really have a problem with PTS.* Not long after that, the Lord showed me that the wives of veterans often had their own PTS. I found that most wives of Vietnam veterans had PTS from childhood sexual abuse, growing up in alcoholic families, traumas such as abortion, rape, and domestic violence. Many Christian women are affected by PTS. Having been a battered wife from my previous marriage, I had a burden to work with women who needed healing. It seemed evident that God was calling me to a ministry of restoration among Christian women. So, I stepped down from my administrative duties at Point Man.

We were camping out at the Point Man annual campout in July of 1991. One morning as I was journaling my prayers, I felt the Lord giving me some direction. He wanted me to be still and learn to listen to His voice. He wanted me to learn to discern His voice from all the others so that I would not be led astray. He wanted me to clearly know His voice so that He could say, *"This is the way, walk ye in it."* I knew then that, by being sensitive to His voice, I would be able to stay on track. I'd then know the difference between a "good idea" and God's idea.

Back in Disobedience

At church one month later, a woman "felt led" to give me a bottle of herbs to help me lose weight without diet or exercise. She let me know that if I liked them and wanted to sell the product she'd help me. Since I was in the ministry, she offered to pay for me to sign up as a distributor.

The product was made up of four herbs, one of which is like a natural form of the drug, "speed." I tried the herbs and my mind began racing and my body bursting with energy. The idea of just sitting at the feet of Jesus lost its appeal. Even though there were medical sources that warned against taking one of the herbs in the formula, it caused such an enthralling feeling that I didn't want to believe it could be dangerous. Of course, there were reassurances from the naturopathic doctor who developed the concoction, and leaders in the multi-level organization that was marketing the product. I chose to listen to those sources who didn't give warnings. I was sold! I felt so good that I didn't bother consulting the Lord. I didn't pray about it. I didn't ask God if I should get involved. It just *seemed right,* so I went for it. After five years in the ministry with limited funds and denying myself luxuries, I was ready to make some money. My direction from the Lord to listen to His voice became a distant memory as the wheels began to turn again.

Chuck stepped down from his position as executive director of Point Man Ministries in August of 1992, a year after I had disobediently jumped back into the business world. He was carrying the burden of the ministry alone and was burned out. There came a time when he really could have used my administrative help, but I was just too busy doing "my thing" to notice that he needed me.

Chuck walked in the door with a frown on his face. He was exhausted from moving the Point Man offices to another building. No one else had come to help him and I was busy with the business.

"Athena, I'm going to stay at the office for a while. I'm not coming home until you make some changes. I just don't think I can handle it anymore. You're not here for me like I need you to be, and either you make some changes or I'm history." After a year of struggling with a wife who was spinning out of control again, he was ready to turn the ministry over to a few of the veteran leaders. His threat got my attention for a little while, but as soon as he came home, things just went back to normal. Finally in desperation, he turned over the ministry and walked away from his calling to Vietnam veterans. He continued to minister to veterans in other countries, but it appeared that his ministry to Vietnam veterans was over. I was part of its undoing. Once I got back on the MLM roller coaster, I quit encouraging him and nurturing him in his ministry and in our marriage. I became self-centered again to the point of being blind to the needs of my husband and family.

Doing the Wrong Thing for the Right Reason

I started losing weight so fast that it seemed too good to be true. Little did I know that using one of the herbs over a long period of time could devastate my adrenal glands and endocrine system.

Quiet times with the Lord were far from my mind as ideas flowed for selling the herbs and all the money I could make. It had been years since I had thought about being money motivated. But after five years in full-time ministry, the idea of having money again was enticing. My money-making days seemed a lifetime away, but I quickly reverted back to that old mentality. *I could help fund Point Man and other ministries*, I thought. I knew what it was like to be on the receiving end, maybe now I could be the one to plant into those who give their lives for the gospel.

Credibility at Work

To build my team with this new product, I began to run recruiting ads on a local Christian radio station. Chuck and I had been interviewed many times on local stations as well as the 700 Club and other national shows. I figured that my credibility in ministry would help open the door to attract honest, hard-working Christians into my business. I had the best of intentions and even believed in my heart that the company I represented had a great product and a wonderful opportunity to offer. My advertisements would plant the idea that working in my business would afford Christians the opportunity to get out of debt, send their children to Christian schools, or even fund ministry projects or missionaries. And I believed that it would!

"Hi, this is Athena Dean," I'd say in my radio ads. "In all my years of business, I've looked for a way to build a business where I could help others achieve their dreams. After five years in full-time ministry, I've realized that most Christians need extra money every month just to get by. But there are other important goals to meet as well. How about getting out of debt or being able to give to ministries and other important missionary efforts? If that is your heart, not buying a "street of dreams" home or winning a pink Cadillac, then give us a call. I'm looking for honest, hardworking, like-minded people who want to make a difference with their lives. I'm building a team of people who will work together to achieve some common goals. If you're interested in earning an extra $500-$2,000 a month part-time, give me a call! I'd love to talk with you!" I spoke encouragingly and convincingly to move listeners to respond.

Wonderful people replied to my ads, and many of them got started with me in my new business. They were people who really loved Jesus and wanted to make some extra money and still feel good about what they were doing. They came from all walks of life, men and women both, some with sales and MLM background, some with none. Three months later when the company went through the first of many crises, I was determined to keep my group going against all odds.

"Have you heard the latest?" It was a call from my upline director. "It seems the doctor ripped off the herbal formula from the manufacturer...he didn't really discover it! It looks like half the company is leaving to start another company right away!" The phone lines were on fire and a large group of distributors began making serious accusations against the leaders of the company. After criticizing the management team, they went off to join companies with copy-cat products.

By this time I already had a lot to protect as my income was up to $2,500 per month. I deafened my ears to all the negatives, protected my group against all the "gossip," and began to defend the founder and the company's reputation. There were three months during the first year when we did not get paid, but I hung in there, never questioning the honesty and integrity of those running the company. Of course, since I was one of the top producers, I always seemed to get preferential treatment. During the three months without pay, I received my pay two of those months so it was easy for me to hang in there and look past the negatives that were slapping everyone else in the face. In my mind, the crisis was just the "enemy" trying to destroy what God was doing. When indications started to crop up that the founder was involved in New Age practices and was in his fourth marriage, I chose to look the other way. I didn't want to believe that I could be wrong. I thought what I believed would override what was coming from the top; that I could influence the company leadership and not be affected myself. Boy, was I wrong.

The Money Rolls In

By the end of my first year, we had weathered three major management turnovers and numerous months when no one got their checks. Many people had left the organization, but I was determined to save the company. I had a vested interest because I had earned over $50,000 that first year.

In January of 1993, I began a mega-blitz of radio ads on local Christian stations as well as many across the country. My income went from $3,500 to $9,500 within four months. From there it continued to climb by $2-3,000 every month. Others in my downline were seeing their income doubling and tripling. We felt our persistence and loyalty was really paying off.

Then Chuck and I had a bright idea. Why not cash in on this big downline and open up a product distribution center for the company? One of our directors offered to put up some of the money as an investment. That led to the idea of creating a corporation and selling stock to selected Christian directors in my downline. It seemed like the perfect way to fund our own training center and make a percentage on the purchases that were already being made by my organization.

And so it began. Those of us involved in the creation of this corporation went to bed at night with more dollar signs dancing in our heads. I had jumped so wholeheartedly into the challenge of this project that Chuck was beginning to have second thoughts.

"I can see it already, Athena. The handwriting is on the wall. This project's only going to eat up even more of your time, time you don't have to spare. Don't do it. I'm warning you, just drop it." Chuck pleaded with me, but we were already too far into the planning process for me to back out. With plans in motion and my adrenaline flowing, the last thing I wanted to do was back off. I disobeyed my husband, and he let me get away it.

Initially, a group of 12 of us met and shared ideas and how we could make it happen. We built many benefits for the shareholders into the agreement. With the growth rate we were experiencing, we felt it would only be a short time before we would all see an incredible profit from our investment. A big motivation was that the distribution center would make it more convenient and easier for us to build our personal downlines. It seemed like a win-win situation.

That first month was exciting. I spent all my time setting up shop in our bright, leased office space. With the shareholders' money, I had a sales counter built, bought furniture, fixtures, signs, and designed four-color sales aids.

It's always easier to spend freely if the money belongs to someone else. My investment in the corporation was to be in "sweat" equity, so I had no cash involved. In those days I was still operating with my own brand of "creative bookkeeping." I had always "robbed Peter to pay Paul," and this time it was no different. When money came in to pay for product, I'd spend it on current necessities rather than setting it aside for more product. I operated without a budget so there was never any way to track expenses and know if we were really on target. *There's plenty of money for everything*, I thought.

That first month we did over $100,000 in business, and the second month we did $175,000. Things were exploding and we felt as if we were sitting on top of the world. We had put together a "class act" and everyone was proud. Good working relationships were building between all the shareholders who took turns working in the office. I really enjoyed coming to work.

"Hi Athena, is there anything I can do for you?" I looked up to see Jo leaning against my office door with a cup of tea. Jo and I had become better acquainted as she helped me organize the office and handled the shareholder correspondence. I counted on her for an honest opinion when I needed someone to talk things over with. We sipped our teas together before the telephone interrupted me again. There wasn't as much time for fellowship as I had thought there would be. Everything was moving so fast.

When one of the other leaders in our company wanted to buy distribution rights to part of the territory in our county, greed kicked in and I moved to buy it for the shareholders. I felt we should have the territory, rather than this unscrupulous Mormon businessman. To swing the purchase of new territory, the shareholders brought in nine additional people from their downlines who were also Christians.

While we were still experiencing growth, we noticed troubling signals from the home office. They began making changes that directly affected our sales. It seemed like they were intentionally trying to cut our profits. Then, after a local newspaper did an exposé on the herbal product we were selling, our business really began to falter. The bad press began to unsettle our customer and distributor base. We tried to rally the troops by refuting the allegations at meetings where we trained them on the "hidden agenda" of the newspaper and the governmental agency involved. Slowly, confidence in the product was beginning to erode among customers and distributors. We made a good case, but we still lost a lot of business.

Ignoring the signals, we continued to operate as if the money was still pouring in. But our monthly sales fluctuated between $100,000 and $140,000 for the next few months — a significant drop. Not wanting to face what was happening, the board of directors and I did not reduce our overhead. I kept hiring office workers to keep up with the added paperwork the home office was requiring. Rather than consult the board, I made decisions on my own and would let them know later, figuring it was easier and faster to get things done that way. I didn't realize I was negating my built-in protective covering from the board, leaving myself wide open for attack. In way over my head, I tried to make the best of a bad situation while still trying to be loyal to the company.

It was October and the company's annual convention time. Putting all my troubling thoughts away for the evening, I anticipated the award I was to receive. I was the first person who would be honored by the esteemed "Ambassador Star Director" position. I dressed carefully in a svelte rich purple dress with sequins that caught the light. In the elegant hotel banquet room, I walked from table to table greeting people and basking in the power and prestige. Two-thirds of the people attending the convention were in my sales organization. Almost all the people going up to the stage to win prizes and be recognized were on my team.

The shareholders had rented a suite in the hotel and hosted a celebration party with hors d'oeuvres and sparkling cider. We posed in all our glitter for a shareholder picture that would be used for our company Christmas card.

"Laura! Come over here and stand with Jana. Let me get a picture of the two of you." Jana was Laura's upline, they were friendly competitors and both top winners in the company contest. Having a glamorous photo to put up on the refrigerator was a great way to keep them both motivated in the future.

We were riding high on our success. Our co-op venture was the talk of the convention and the shareholders still felt exuberant about the future. It was a heady feeling. While we were all Christians and giving the Lord credit for the success, there was still a lot of pride, arrogance and flesh in control. We were the "Dean Team" and felt superior to the other organizations within the company because we were so righteous and honest. We were elitists, giving off airs of being special. That night at the convention, the spotlight definitely was on income, worldly success and recognition.

The very next month the company decided to make a major change in the compensation plan that decreased the pay of our hard workers by 50 percent. My worst nightmare was coming true.

"Athena, I don't understand," said Laura with panic in her voice. "My check is down by $2,000. What is going on?"

"Laura, it must be a mistake. Maybe sales were down more than we realized. I'll call the office and find out what's up. I'm sure it's nothing to worry about," I reassured her.

As I hung up the phone I felt a tiny tug of fear. Maybe I had been in denial about this company. My stomach felt like lead as I dialed the number of the home office. I began to pray, "Oh God, don't let this be another management crisis." To my questions, I got double-talk back. The company's management team was executing a well-laid plan of deception and intimidation. The people I trusted and defended had failed me and my organization. Maybe the negative comments about the company I had heard in the past were true. How could I possibly go on promoting the integrity of this company after it had become obvious to me that they were dishonest and unethical? I felt betrayed and used — as if my face had been slapped. Still, I sought frantically for a way to make it work.

In the months that followed it became clear to me that I had made a terrible mistake in judgment. Because of our credibility, many other Christians had followed us and committed to representing a company that not only had unethical leadership, but products that were not entirely safe.

I was not yet at the point of realizing my own disobedience in even being involved. In my heart I knew that I had condoned questionable actions and ignored red flags to protect my own empire. I saw that we had no future with this company and started looking for another company to represent. Uppermost in my thoughts was protecting the shareholders of our co-op and having another option to offer my downline. Even though we were a group of Christians who professed to believe in prayer, we were still trying to handle the situation ourselves.

As I began to vocalize my disappointment with the company and their lack of integrity, dissention began to rise up in our co-op. There were those in the ranks who were still loyal to the company and blamed me only for the financial problems. To protect our investments, the board of directors was in agreement with finding other types of income. However, a handful of shareholders did not agree.

Putting a Bandaid on a Bullet Hole

We rushed into another business to try to keep the ball rolling. A friend of ours who was in full-time ministry sent Chuck and me information on a large Canadian company that had recently launched its product line in the U.S. using multi-level marketing as their distribution method. This company dealt in high-tech communications products with a high price tag. An excellent product, the sound financial management, and the company's integrity were attractive after our past experience. The video presentation sold us and we quickly got the rest of the team together to take a look at the new opportunity. I didn't really pray about the new company. It just sounded like a good alternative and the potential for making money sounded good.

I spent the next six months consumed by trying to build the same glorious reputation and track record with the new company, filling up that need in my own heart for recognition and importance. It was like putting a bandaid on a bullet hole. Not only was the method the problem, but so were my motives.

This move to add on another company and product created more disunity among the shareholders and rumors began to fly. The herbal product company knew I would no longer defend them and their actions, so it was only a matter of time before they found a way to get rid of me. My contract was terminated for getting involved with another company. Determined to save the shareholder's investments, I resigned from the board of directors so the co-op could continue to provide product to the local distributors. To those who had stayed loyal to the company, I had become the enemy. I was losing control and began to get very defensive at the thought of my friends turning against me.

I felt anxious and uncertain. The dream we had built was starting to slip through my fingers and I hated the feeling of things being out of control.

It wasn't long before the co-op got confirmation about documented cases of people getting sick on the product. When they went to the company to demand a recall of particular lot numbers, the company refused to take responsibility. At the same time, we verified that the company had dropped its liability insurance that automatically covered the distributors. This was the last straw.

The deception and intimidation from the company quickly brought us out of the denial we had been in for some time. With what we felt was righteous indignation, we decided we could no longer, in good conscience, keep selling the product to distributors now that we knew the truth. Quietly, the board of directors moved to terminate our contract with the herbal company. We notified the shareholders of our intentions to sell all assets and cash all the shareholders out. Those of us who were in agreement on promoting the new communications business out of the same location planned on making this new venture a way to recoup our losses. Everyone was taking a huge loss. I felt hollow inside as we sold off all the assets to raise the cash for the final dissolution of the corporation. Still feeling responsible for the huge losses, I was determined to make it right somehow.

It was devastating to watch the deterioration of this group of believers. Friends were now enemies. People who used to drop in daily just to fellowship now steered clear of the center. Conversations that used to be filled with joy, prayer and love for one another were now chillingly polite. We had come together as Christians, but our overriding motive was the desire to make money. When the money was gone, many of the relationships were also gone. Friends were bickering. People who used to talk on the phone every day were suddenly icy cold to each other. The love of money proved to be a deadly poison for relationships.

S I X

Fatal Attractions

I can clearly see the deceptive traps I fell into. My way of getting recognition was by making myself indispensable. I would do the job bigger and better than anyone ever had so the company I represented would need me. I had been well trained to verbally magnify people's strong points in order to motivate them to increase their sales volume. At meetings my technique was to call people up on the stage and tell the audience how special and motivated and talented they were. The building up they should have been getting from home they all-too-often got from me. Some of the men with whom I worked began to need me more than their wives!

Because my husband was involved in ministry, I was a lone ranger in running my business. I was doing my thing and he was doing his. All Chuck cared about was getting people saved. All I cared about was getting people involved in my business. When faced with needs in other's lives, Chuck focused on what he could do to glorify God. He was concerned about where the people he met would spend eternity. My conversations revolved around the exciting business I was in. This didn't feel strange to me, as I was still denying my own pain and using my work as an anesthetic. Because I was out of the biblical order for husband

and wife relationships; I was no longer under the protection of the spiritual head of our household. I did whatever I wanted, whenever I wanted, without consulting Chuck. This left me wide open to error because I was ignoring the spiritual covering that God had placed in my life.

I would wake up every morning with my wheels turning. Usually I was too busy and running too late for much prayer and Bible study in the mornings. Any prayer time that I did cram in was just a long list of wants and needs and thanksgiving for financial blessings. I never stopped long enough to listen to His voice and get His orders for the day. I certainly did not spend enough time with the Lord to allow Him to convict me when I was in error!

Because of my lack of Christian disciplines and time spent listening to God's voice, I was susceptible to ungodly suggestions. It felt good to have other men build me up and flatter me. I sensed suggestions from the enemy that intimate relationships with other men in the same business could really be exciting! I was so driven and consumed by my business and need for recognition through what I could accomplish, that I was a prime target.

It is well known that power, sex and money are the temptations that derail the fruitful ministries of on-fire pastors and Christian leaders. These are also the three main intoxicants of the business world. Perhaps 70 percent of those involved in multi-level organizations are women, but many of those who train, motivate and lead these organizations are men. Could it be that multi-level marketing and other free enterprise systems attract those women who are needy and longing for someone to make them feel good about themselves?

Melanie was so motivated by sales contests that she'd deprive herself of sleep, working long hours, just to be recognized a winner. She grew up with alcoholic parents, and never received the love or nurturing as a child that she so desperately needed. She did everything she could to keep the verbal affirmations coming from her network marketing company.

God designed men and women to be attracted to one another. When the men who are paid to "motivate the troops" begin to compliment women and encourage them in their businesses, the dynamics change and the law of attraction kicks in.

The problem isn't only with those who are running the show either. I can't tell you how many times I've seen women, single and married, fall for men with whom they are involved in business. With so much in common and long hours spent together, before long they begin to bond.

A friend of mine was a casualty in this area. Marnie had a strong walk with the Lord. She discipled me when I was just beginning to learn to surrender to Jesus. Her marriage was going through hard times as her husband was serving time in prison. Even while they were separated, their relationship was strong and they both loved the Lord. I always admired her strength and their commitment to one another. We had renewed our relationship when we saw each other at a meeting and she became part of my organization and a top producer for the company. Since I tried to make myself indispensable, we were rewarded with time spent strategizing with the "big boys" who ran the company. One of them, a professing Christian, was an incredibly smooth-talking, motivational, dynamic, good-looking man from the South. Nathan watched out for our interests and made sure we got preferential treatment. He spent a lot of time "selling the dream" to us. There was definitely some bonding going on between us all. We would go out for dessert after the evening meetings and talk, laugh, cry and dream together for hours into the night. It wasn't long before Marnie and Nathan began spending time alone together. Marnie quit visiting her husband in prison, and that was the end of her marriage.

Deceived

I couldn't believe she could be so blind! How dare she fall for the trap that the enemy had set? Surely she was stronger and wiser than that! 1 Corinthians 10:12 says *"Therefore, let him who thinks he stands take heed, lest he fall."* It wasn't more than 30 days after I criticized my friend for her lack of discernment that I began to be sucked into the same trap. I had lost a lot of weight and was enjoying getting compliments and attention. Part of the fun was buying attractive new clothes for the new me. One pantsuit I had bought in a quality department store was my favorite as it made me look especially thin. When I wore it I'd look in the mirror and smile remembering one guy's offhand comment, "Man, Athena....you sure are lookin' good these days! If I weren't married, you'd be in trouble!"

Chuck was out of town a lot, speaking to veterans' groups. He traveled to Russia to minister to the veterans and their families of the war in Afghanistan. I was so wrapped up in "my thing" that I felt we didn't have too much in common anymore. When I started traveling frequently on my own, one of the new big wigs from the company began to play me for all I was worth. Perry would call me on the phone two or three times a day to see how he could help me with my business. He would ask me questions about me and my life, and how I got to be such a winner. I'm sure his strategy was to strengthen my devotion to the company so my sales volume would continue to grow. He made me feel important and needed. When he crossed the line from business to flirting, I didn't even notice.

I found myself seated across from Perry in the restaurant of our conference hotel. Three of us were relaxing after a big meeting, talking excitedly about our futures with the company. Perry looked at me and said, "Athena...you did a great job tonight! If it weren't for your leadership, I don't know what we would do." He paused, looked steadily into my eyes and said, "You sure do have nice eyes," and winked.

Soon I was consumed with thinking about how I could impress him with my wit, talents and looks. *I'll make sure he sees what a leader I am.* I would try to make sure I was at meetings where he would be and we orchestrated our schedules so that he would be where I was teaching or training. By God's grace, I did not commit physical adultery, but we all know the Scripture found in Matthew 5:28: *If you've done it in your mind, you've done it.*

Chuck sensed that I was drifting away and finally he confronted me. "Athena, something's up. Things don't seem right between us and you know it. You've never been able to keep things from me. So what is it?"

I couldn't hide it any longer. With tears, I confessed my sin.

"Oh Chuck...I've crossed the line. I don't know how it happened, but I've bonded with Perry and I know that I'm in a dangerous position. You've got to help me."

In the days to follow, Chuck and I retraced the steps leading to my deception. We spent three months going over the subtle decisions and choices I made that took me down the wrong road. We looked at every step so in the future I'd be able to foresee my areas of vulnerability. I realized then that as soon as I had quit praying everyday and getting into the Word, spending quality quiet time at Jesus' feet and listening for His voice, my ability to discern good from evil crashed. I praise God that I have a husband who is understanding enough to help me set boundaries and who loves me enough to forgive.

I learned firsthand why focusing on success can be so dangerous to a Christian. The tendency is to become so consumed that even our devotion to Jesus takes second place. When that happens, making the wrong choices is inevitable.

I was not in the Word enough to pay attention to the warnings of 1 Timothy 6:6-11.

But godliness with contentment is great gain. For we brought nothing into this world, and it is certain we can carry nothing out. And having food and clothing, with these we shall be content. But those who desire to be rich fall into temptation and a snare, and into many foolish and harmful lusts which drown men in destruction and perdition. For the love of money is a root of all kinds of evil, for which some have strayed from the faith in their greediness, and pierced themselves through with many sorrows. But you, O man of God, flee these things and pursue righteousness, godliness, faith, love, patience, gentleness.

I didn't see that Scripture as pertaining to me, but always to someone else. I did not give Jesus time to convict my heart on a daily basis. Because of that, my heart was hard as stone.

The truth is, I allowed my business to draw me away from my husband. The business had *become* my husband. I had become vulnerable to emotional infidelity because of it. The business was the place I got my strokes, my warm fuzzies. It became my family. I nurtured and paid more attention to those in my business than I did my own children.

Our daughter, Roby, who is now 25, told me recently how, as a sophomore, she ran for class officer at Bothell High School. As she was telling me about the incredible speech that she had given at the opening assembly at school, I thought to myself, *You missed it. Where were you when she was growing up?* I hadn't even known what was going on in her life.

I kept so busy that I had no clue what our kids were doing and what was really going on in their lives. I just kept promising my kids that same lie that I had bought: "Someday when we are making enough money, I'll slow down on the business and spend more time with you!" Of course, that day never came. No matter how much I made, I was still consumed by making more. It was easier for me to spend my time at business rather than building relationships with my children and spouse. It gives me sorrow to say that at this time, three of our four kids love the world more than they love the Lord. Much of that, I feel, is due to all my broken promises and years of putting my business ahead of my family. I can count at least ten family vacations that never happened or were cancelled at the last minute because of my work. This happened so many times that I'm sure it got to be a bad joke.

I looked up from my work at the clock. My son, Garrett, who was 11 years old at the time, was three hours late getting home from football practice. *I was supposed to pick him up!* I was frantic! Chuck had left with the car and there wasn't anyone I could call.

About fifteen minutes later, a devastated Garrett walked in the door. He had sat in front of the high school football field and waited, and waited, and waited. He was sure every car that turned the corner toward the school was mine. With each car that passed him by, his heart broke a little more. He was chilled as the sky grew dark, but he kept on waiting for his mom. For some reason, the coach came back by the field and saw him waiting there at 8 o'clock at night.

I've asked him to forgive me, but the impact of my blatant negligence on his young life haunts me. Garrett is one who got his emotional needs met by the mothering of his friends' moms when he was a pre-teen. When he became a teenager, he bonded with his friends. I missed so much by not being available for him.

Ailen was seven when I married his father. I never really bonded with him, and in reaction, he shut himself off emotionally from his new mom. He always seemed serious with anger boiling beneath the surface. I'm sure part of that anger was because I acted as if he didn't even exist. I just let Chuck parent him and didn't pay much attention to him at all. After all, I hardly paid any attention to my own kids, let alone a stepchild.

My youngest, Aaron, has become very money-motivated himself, always focusing on the things money can buy. Just to be close to me, he would flop on my bed while I worked away in my bedroom and page through catalogues, all the while talking about what he wanted to buy. I'd half-heartedly say, "Great, Aaron, go for it." But I hardly ever really heard what he was saying. When he was young, I'd buy him off by giving him things instead of my time and my heart.

Chasing the "American Dream" has taken an awful toll on families. Women who aren't getting their needs met at home or who have experienced tremendous wounding in their lives seem to be attracted to this type of business. I've seen many women who were unconsciously coping with latent pain by spending most of their time being busy. I was also one of those wounded women. Consumed with building a business, the Lord never had a chance to walk me through the healing I so desperately needed.

Betty was also a motivated over-achiever. Growing up in a large family, she had to compete for attention. At the dinner table, she would have to yell at the top of her lungs just to get a word in edgewise. She continued to be rejected over and over in her life, and she saw MLM as her way to get the recognition she needed to feel good about herself again.

It All Came
Crashing Down

In June of 1994, I saw Chuck off at the airport for his flight to Virginia Beach where he was attending the Christian Broadcasting Network's annual Victory Over Vietnam Conference. I was glad he was getting away as I thought for sure God had something to say to Chuck about the restoration of his vision for his ministry to Vietnam veterans.

God had a different agenda. His plan in sending Chuck to CBN was to get me alone for a whole weekend so He could put His finger on some areas of sin in my life! He needed my full attention so He could begin to convict me on my heart motives.

For the first time in years, I was feeling an overwhelming urge to pray. Prayer was my last resort these days. But that weekend, as I quietly spent time in prayer, the Lord took me back to July of 1991. I felt compelled to dig out that journal entry. As I reread the marching orders the Lord had given me, I felt a wave of conviction wash over me. For the first time in three years, I was confronted with the strong feeling that I had been in complete disobedience by getting back into MLM. It was as clear as the ink scrawls in my journal. God had told me what He wanted me to do and I had not obeyed. I had gone off in another direction, just because it sounded good! I had assumed that, because I saw an open door, I should go through it. The Lord was making it undeniably clear that just because that door was open did not mean He wanted me to walk through it!

God's Convicting Power

The new high-tech communication business that we had jumped into seemed to have all the ingredients that the other company lacked. But the Lord was showing me that motives, not good management or great products, were the issue at heart. To get started in the new business, distributors would have to spend anywhere from $1,500 to $5,000. We encouraged people to use their credit cards — to go into debt — to get their business going.

That weekend before the Lord I was feeling stressed and anxious as I thought of the struggle we were having to rebuild our organizations with a new product and company. The new business was not growing as fast as it needed to in order to cover all the overhead of the office space where we had kept our training center. For the first time in three years, I was unsure enough of myself to stop and listen to God. Immediately, He directed me to a book in the bookcase called *Men's Manual: Financial Freedom* by Bill Gothard. Thinking I'd find some suggestions for the problem of insufficient finances, I turned to the section of the book on financial freedom principles. The words I read pierced my heart.

Gothard listed God's four purposes for money:
1) to provide basic needs
2) to confirm direction
3) to give to Christians
4) to illustrate God's power.[1]

Purpose number two jumped off the page at me. *"Money, or lack thereof, is God's way of confirming His direction for our lives."*[2]

If people used credit to get involved in our new business, they were bypassing God's caution sign. If the money wasn't available, that was His way of saying no! We were suggesting and even encouraging Christians to "make it happen" on their own without God's blessing or confirmation.

My heart was heavy with conviction as I continued to look through Bill Gothard's book. In the section on "Developing Sales Resistance," I found a definition that brought me godly sorrow.

SALES RESISTANCE
Being content with food and clothing, using
and caring for the possessions that we have,
and keeping our focus on the purpose for
which God made us.[3]

Gothard defined alluring advertising as "Carefully planned appeals to our human weaknesses designed to make us discontent with what we have so that we can rationalize buying things that we know we do not need and should not have."[4]

At that moment the most powerful conviction I have ever felt swept over me. The previous three years were like a weight on my back. I knew right then that I had been full of rebellion, disobedience, and sin. As I read on, the Lord showed me all the different ways I was promoting sinful behavior in the ways I did my business. Gothard's list of subtle advertising tactics included the following:

Creating discontentment

Promoting an independent spirit

Depending on human reasoning

Appealing to the lust of the eyes

Offering fulfillment apart from God

Denying the product's weakest point.[5]

That is exactly what we were doing in our business, and in every sales business I'd ever been involved with! As the weight of what I had done began to press down on me, I felt so ashamed. The Lord did an instant replay of every advertisement I'd ever written for the radio ad campaigns. He reminded me of every script I'd ever written for the voice mail message people would hear when they called in for information. He took me back to the way I'd written the slide show presentation and every other sales tool I had created. I saw those tactics in every promotional campaign I had ever done, even after I became a Christian. My conscience had been activated and I could no longer compromise or straddle the fence by being deceitful or dishonest.

But God wasn't done with me yet. He began to show me how I had been using my God-given ability to inspire and motivate people for the wrong ends. I was using my gifts to encourage people to make money and build a successful business, rather than inspiring them to a closer walk with Jesus.

Facing the Obvious

The next Monday morning I was sitting in my office feeling emotionally wrung out when Jo walked in. She looked at me with concern and said, "Can we go to lunch? I know you have lots on your mind; maybe it'll help to talk."

I knew that God had sent her and that I was going to have to spill out all that God had been showing me. I was so used to being the strong one, the leader for everyone, I felt I was taking a risk in exposing my heart, but I knew Jo's sensitivity to the things of God and felt she would not condemn me.

As we were going through the buffet line at the pizza place down the street, I was feeling confused and nervous about exposing what God had shown me. But I couldn't turn back now. I blurted out what the Lord had been revealing. Tears ran down my cheeks and I mopped them up with the napkins at the table. I felt overwhelmed with godly sorrow and saw my sin the way God looks at sin.

Along with my sorrow, I was feeling terribly conflicted. "I can't let the shareholders down. I have to keep it together so people won't lose their investment. I have to keep on being the leader and motivating the troops." Even as I said those words, they sounded foolish in my ears. *How could I control everything when God wants to be in control?*

Jo made me face the obvious, "Give it up, Athena. You cannot try to save the corporation or keep the things going if God is shutting the door. Why don't you just let God do whatever He wants to do?"

The new business was not making enough money to meet the overhead of our 2,400-square-foot office now that we no longer had the profits from the herbal product.

"Get rid of the office," she offered, "scale back, just let it grow slowly and see what God does."

I was used to doing business with flair and pizazz, being everything to everyone, and being the best of the best. To do what she suggested almost seemed impossible. My palms became sweaty and I felt a knot in my stomach. Letting go of the control I had was frightening, yet as I entertained the thought, I felt a burden roll off my shoulders. I thought about it for hours. When I picked Chuck up from the airport, I told him all about what had been happening to me and what the Lord was showing me. After I had gotten it all out, I asked him what he thought. "Shut it down!" He wholeheartedly agreed.

How was I going to tell my associates what I was feeling? I knew they wouldn't all be as understanding as Jo was. I was going to quit being their leader and going to let God direct the course of the business and it's outcome. I was no longer going to make things happen. No writing the monthly newsletter, holding opportunity meetings, overseeing training sessions, organizing cooperative advertising programs, and generally making things happen.

I finally let go of my responsibility to save people's investments. This decision hadn't come without excruciating emotional pain. I kept thinking, *How can I abandon everyone? How can I let my people down? How can I walk away?*

The Lord just kept reassuring me, *Let it go. You have to let it go.* Finally, I gave up being responsible for everyone else and decided to be obedient to what I felt God was showing me I had to do.

As the ground rules changed, people's real motives became clear. Making a profit was really the bottom line of everything we had created, and people were just the means to that end, including me. It was at that moment that I clearly saw the fruit of a vow I made when I was nineteen years old.

After falling in love at 19, I had been badly hurt and had felt taken advantage of and used. When the relationship ended, I said to myself, *I will never let anyone use me again.* When I made that decision, I hardened my heart and unconsciously set out to live my life in line with that vow.

The results of my vow were powerful in my life. In order to never allow anyone to use me, the pendulum swung and I became the user. I felt I must control every situation at all costs and I must not allow myself to be vulnerable to others. After all, I had found out that people could not be trusted, so I would make sure I never got hurt again.

The Lord revealed to me that I had been using others and they had been using me. I had used those shareholders to make myself look good and make money and they were using me and my leadership talents to make lots of money as well. Now that I was drawing a boundary and saying, "No more; I will not be your leader; I will not lead you into the promised land; I will not play the same role I have played for the last three years..." there were hard feelings.

Seven of us sat in a circle. I had pulled back from active participation in the meetings and questions were being asked. I couldn't put it off any longer. I had to tell the board that I was finished and let them know what I thought we ought to do with the center.

"I'm sorry you guys. I just can't do it any more. I think we need to close this place down and just see what happens. You will all have to take up the slack, take care of your people, and run your own meetings. I didn't want to let you down, but I just feel like this is what the Lord is asking me to do," I painfully explained.

Their faces registered dismay, worry, and shock. I had a settled peace that what I was doing what was right, so I didn't give in and try to make everyone feel better by saying I'd take care of it. It was a relief to have that meeting over with.

This was a very difficult time for all of us as our future was uncertain. I wasn't even sure who I was anymore, for my identity had been so wrapped up in my leadership position and those I worked with.

The World's Redemption

I was scheduled to attend a leadership training session in Palm Springs for the high-tech company with which I was working. By this time I knew the Lord didn't want me involved in any way at all, but I couldn't get out of the commitment because the company had paid my way.

As I sat in the back of the room during the final phase of the training, I felt sick to my stomach. I clearly understood the abomination of the business methods that I had involved myself with. Each leader was to stand up in front of the rest of the room and practice his or her inspirational speech on the audience. Then we were to go back to our teams and motivate them to greater achievements in the months to come. Of course, this would result in more income for us.

It was Sunday morning and I was keenly aware that I was not in church worshipping, but in a room full of people, many of them Christians, who were worshipping the almighty dollar. Feeling disconnected, I watched and listened to a former pastor stand up and "share his heart."

"This is the most incredible opportunity you will ever have a chance to be a part of," he said. "This is a chance for you to make your dreams come true! We're at a place in time that is like none other. You cannot afford to let this chance pass you by. It could, and literally will, change your whole life. I want to look back and be able to tell my grand-children that I made a difference in this world. With this company, I'll be able to say that with conviction and hon-esty. And you can, too! Don't wait. Don't delay. Don't drag your feet, because this train is a-movin' and you won't want to be left behind!"

If I didn't know any better, I'd think he was preaching to the faithful. He was preaching, but it was the world's redemption — fame, fortune and success. I stayed in the back row and let one of the other leaders from our group do the speech for us. I felt sick and shrank down in my chair and prayed it would be over quickly. Running through my head was my prayer to the Lord, *Oh God, forgive us for being so deceived!*

Yes, it all came crashing down. My successful ways of doing business, my standard operating procedure that had made us thousands upon thousands of dollars, was exposed by the holiness of God. I knew then that there was no go-ing back. No matter what our financial condition, I never again wanted anything in my life that was not God's per-fect will. I had lived my life with one good idea after an-other, and many of them paid off. But just because they made money, were they God's ideas for my life? Were they God's ideas for the others I got involved? Again, that Scrip-ture crashed through my mind, *"There is a way that seems right to a man, but its end is the way of death"* (Prov. 14:12).

I could now see clearly that just because a door was opened to me didn't mean I was supposed to walk through it. Because I didn't commit to prayer and wait for confirmation and peace, seeking godly counsel from those to whom I was accountable, I was wide open for deception. And deceived I was. Those three years of disobedience almost cost me my marriage, my children, my spiritual life, my integrity. But praise God, His mercies are new every morning.

> *If we say that we have fellowship with Him, and walk in darkness, we lie and do not practice the truth. But if we walk in the light as He is in the light, we have fellowship with one another, and the blood of Jesus Christ His Son cleanses us from all sin. If we say we have no sin, we deceive ourselves, and the truth is not in us. If we confess our sins, He is faithful and just to forgive us our sins and cleanse us from all unrighteousness* (1 John 1:6-9).

My Deliverance

After returning home from Palm Springs, I went through three long months of depression and confusion. God had ripped out of me the motivation to make money and I felt useless. I did not have a mission in life, I felt like a loser and a fraud. There were many days where I would still be in my blue bathrobe at 3:00 in the afternoon, my hair still a mess, my eyes void of any life at all. People constantly called, asking me what was wrong.

"Athena! Where have you been? I thought for sure you would be at the meeting last night! Were you sick or something?" I couldn't explain what I still didn't really have a grasp of, so I just told people that I was taking a leave of absence to deal with some family problems. That seemed to keep people happy and made them more understanding about my lack of involvement.

What I was really feeling was guilt and remorse for the way I had done business. I knew I could no longer promote this "road to success." If God had made it clear that I could no longer be involved in any form of MLM, then how could I encourage others to get involved? I began to try to gracefully back out of the situation I was in. I was on the advisory council for the communications company, an esteemed leadership committee that practically ran the entire show. Every other week we would have nationwide two-and three-hour conference calls. It was nearly impossible for me to drag myself out of bed for those calls. I was just emotionally decimated. I had no strength, no interest in the business, no desire to compete or achieve or impress anyone. I felt hollow and phony and had absolutely nothing to offer. Soon I refused to speak on the phone or see anyone. Chuck had to take care of all the household chores.

There were times in those bleak months when Jo came by in the middle of the day to find me lying on the couch in my bathrobe, immobilized. She would talk with me and cry out to God for me, praying for me when I was too depressed to pray for myself. Sensing the dark night of the soul that I was in, she stood in the gap on my behalf.

Gradually, I felt a little stronger and began to cry out to God for myself:

"Oh, God...cause me to hate the things that You hate, and love the things that You love!"

"Cause me to be excited about Your kingdom, not worldly projects and ventures."

"Cause me to value relationships and people for what and who they are, not for what I can get out of them."

"Remove the stronghold in my life that has caused me to love the things of this world more than I love You!"

God answered those prayers.

One sunny day in late August I closed myself in my bedroom, lay on my bed and sobbed uncontrollably for hours. I wailed at the top of my lungs. The pain was so intense I could hardly stand it. But when it was over, I felt cleansed and different. It was as if something that was lodged inside my being had been removed, stripped out, gone for good. In its place was a peace, a fulfillment, a true longing for the things of God. I had been transformed by the power of the Holy Spirit of God. My urge to jump out there and be important was gone. I could actually listen for God's will and be obedient, without compulsive, dysfunctional behavior getting in the way. God had truly done a new work in me, and I was amazed.

During my three months of darkness, Chuck picked up the slack by rustling up photography and book publishing jobs. Previously he had spent his time ministering to veterans on the computer, writing, and not worrying much about our income. It was a miracle that we were able to pay our substantial house payments each month as my income dwindled away to nothing. I would try to help him during this time, but I wasn't worth much.

Tentmaking Together

As I felt ready to face working again, Chuck and I took a season of prayer and fasting at home. We cried out to God to show us what we should do to pay our bills. Kneeling together at the edge of our bed we pleaded with the Lord, "Oh God, please show us Your will for our lives!"

He made it very clear that He wanted us to work together as a couple. He brought the thought to my mind that, if I just helped Chuck in the publishing end of things, we could make enough money to pay the bills. Instead of blurting it out to him, I waited to see if the Lord would speak the same thing to Chuck's heart. Within a day or two, Chuck came to me and said, "I feel like the Lord wants us to just focus on the publishing business. We need to work together. No more 'lone ranger' stuff."

As a team we could be useful to the Lord and generate the income we needed to live. He put a deep desire in our hearts to see the Word of God in action in people's lives by means of the printed page. This meant that we should narrow our focus down to working specifically with Christian writers. Helping Christians self-publish their testimonies, teachings or personal experiences in book form would be our ministry and would provide for our family. We had published 12 books or so over the previous seven years, some while we were in the ministry and others where we helped friends self-publish their books on the side. This was something we could do full-time from our home, be here for the children, and serve the Body of Christ. We established rates that were 25-50 percent less than the competition, and could still make a living. I wouldn't get consumed, and we would be instrumental in getting the good news out and touching people's lives.

We now work with our hands and our minds in Christian publishing. We work five days a week, six to eight hours a day from our home, but we are available to stop and focus in on our teenagers and young adults when needed. It is amazing to see how God is restoring our relationships with our children, as well as their faith in Him.

Roby Hears the Still, Small Voice

Our eldest daughter, Roby, has been backsliding ever since she got saved after Christmas in 1986. We were so busy doing our thing back then, that we didn't really nurture her and disciple her in the ways of God. We really didn't even know how. Because she never learned how to hear God's voice, it was easy for the enemy to deceive her. There was a huge wedge between us, especially when we really walked away from the world and sold out for Jesus.

As the Lord began to turn my heart toward my children, I began to diligently intercede for Jesus to make Himself real to them in such a way that they could no longer deny Him. Chuck and I would daily cry out to God for Him to draw our children back to Himself.

Just before Christmas of 1995, Roby hit the skids. She had spent a year in the Caribbean running from God and now she was in Santa Barbara trying to find happiness in the world. The Lord had stripped her of everything. She had no job, no car, no future. Everything was falling apart. As she tearfully told Chuck on the phone what was happening, he said, "Come on home, honey. You can stay here as long as you need to."

We had just finished publishing Robert Andrew's excellent book entitled *The Family, God's Weapon for Victory*. Reading it, we had both been convicted that we had not protected our daughter from the enemy's ploy to pull her away from the Lord. Now, we wanted to do what we could to create an environment of restoration.

At first when Roby came home, she was distant and hesitant. She didn't want to be preached to. She just wanted to get back on her feet. Through a series of circumstances, the Lord spoke to her in ways no man could orchestrate. She *knew* God was calling her name. She could no longer run. He was making Himself real to her. Her heart softened and she recommitted her life to the Lord shortly after Christmas.

But she continued to struggle. The enemy fought hard to gain back the ground he had lost. One night we were sitting up in the living room, talking about the things of the Lord. Chuck and I began to share with Roby how important it is to hear God's voice. She began to ask us questions about how we know when we are hearing His voice.

"Roby, it's that still, small voice you hear inside your heart. It's not some audible voice that booms down from the clouds. It can sometimes even seem like it's your voice talking, but you can feel it in your heart, that He is speaking," Chuck explained. Her eyes lit up as she exclaimed, "Oh that's His voice! I never realized it before!" She couldn't wait to get down to her room so she could have a conversation with the Lord.

What we saw happen over the next few days was nothing short of miraculous. Her countenance was completely transformed. She was a new person. The nervous anxiety was gone. She was filled with that peace that passes all understanding. She basked in the love that Jesus poured into her. He told her how much He loves her and that He has a plan for her life. Jesus made Himself completely real to our daughter. Oh, what a joy to see our prayers answered and her life transformed. She is growing by leaps and bounds and her spiritual walk is deepening by the day. The Lord is using her to minister to our other children and I have hope that He will do the same for them. Our God is truly able!

With our new working situation we are able to volunteer in different ministry projects at our local church. Every month God brings in enough publishing jobs to pay the bills. We don't do extravagant promotional campaigns to get business, we just put the word out in various areas and let the Lord direct people to us. We turn away manuscripts that may bring dishonor to the Lord, even if we need the money. God always honors our integrity and sends us another job right away. He is so faithful and provides for us as we trust and obey. He gives us creative ways to earn money and moves mountains when we depend on Him instead of our own ideas.

> *For my thoughts are not your thoughts, nor are your ways my ways, says the Lord. For as the heavens are higher than the earth, so are my ways higher than your ways, and my thoughts than your thoughts* (Isaiah 55:8-9).

The Lord has taught us that in everything we do we must check our heart motives. We cannot operate in gray areas. Everything we do must be able to stand up to his holiness. We must walk in the light as He is in the light. He has convicted me that I must wait for Him to provide at all times. I cannot do my traditional "creative bookkeeping" by robbing Peter to pay Paul. I must be faithful in the small things and wait for Him to show Himself strong.

If there's no business coming in, God is usually trying to get my attention. I've learned to say, "Lord, what are You saying? What are You trying to tell me?" There is usually something I need to repent of or some totally unrelated area that He wants to purify. Somehow, the lack of money always brings me to my knees.

I've learned that just because the world would say that we should use our 90-day line of credit and float money and checks, spending money designated for printing for salaries and then hustling to get more business to pay the printer later, doesn't mean we should. He has convicted me that there are no gray areas. God has us on a short leash, and we must conduct all our affairs in righteousness and holiness.

SECTION II

"Do I Have a Deal for You!"

EIGHT

Preying Not Praying

I was a born-again, Spirit-filled believer, but my spiritual disciplines had gone down the drain. I had no hunger for God's Word and hardly ever prayed. I was a lukewarm Christian, but I knew all the right lingo to sound like a solid believer.

"What a blessing this business is! God has given me an opportunity to help others help themselves! How wonderful to be able to minister to those who need our product!" My heart was hard as stone, but my livelihood was derived from selling other believers on my "way of life." All I could think about were new ways to get more people in the Body of Christ involved in my business. I wasn't praying, I was *preying.* I had so many people at my church involved in my business, that going to church was almost like going to work.

I would look around during praise and worship and notice someone who seemed to be the type of person who would do well in the business. Then I would notice someone else struggling with a weight problem. Pretty soon, everyone I looked at in church was a prospect! During the fellowship time after the service, someone always approached me about the business.

"Athena, I want you to meet someone! She's having great success with the product and is interested in getting the business going."

There was always something related to business that came up before, during, or after the service. Inevitably, someone would need some product or paperwork which I conveniently had in my car. I loved going to retreats, Bible studies and church meetings because someone would always ask me what I did and that would open the door for me to sell or recruit them. This was especially true once my name and voice were blaring on Christian radio.

"Oh, *you're* Athena Dean! I hear your ad every morning driving to work! Does that stuff really work?" I loved it when people recognized my name. I felt like a celebrity! When our commercials ran during the primetime "Wheel of Fortune" program on a major Seattle television station, it was even more enthralling!

With all the publicity, it was a natural that any Christian event I attended would be fertile ground for adding to my numbers. I was convinced that my herbal product was great for people, so I ignored everything negative about it in the press or from unhappy customers. I had convinced myself that I was doing them a favor. My heart motives were glazed over with a misguided missionary zeal to help others help themselves.

Now when I read in Jeremiah 17:9-10 where it says,

The heart is deceitful above all things, and desperately wicked; who can know it? I, the Lord, search the heart, I test the mind, even to give every man according to his ways, and according to the fruit of his doings.

I remember how deceived my heart was. We easily justify what we are doing before men, but God knows our hearts. He will judge us according to our ways and the fruit of our doings. That is a scary thought if you're where I was.

Preying On-Line

I have been amazed at the on-line recruiting schemes that are perpetrated in the name of Christ. I recently took a stroll through the Christianity OnLine bulletin board named "Business Opportunities" and was shocked at what I found.

One headline read, "MAKE LOTS OF CASH" and went on to read, "Make $100,000 in 60 days...just think what good you could do, to the glory of God."

All you have to do is send an e-mail message to this guy and he'll get you the details. When you request the details, you receive a file named BIGBUCKS. It is, very simply, an on-line chain letter. To sign up in the program you put cash in ten envelopes and send them to the ten names on the list. Not only are chain letters illegal, but they also violate U.S. postal regulations as they are considered to be gambling.

Another headline read, "65-cent Tape Can Make U Rich!" The text of the ad read: "Nothing could be simpler! People all over the country are earning $500, $1,000, $10,000 — as much as $100,000 per month doing this part-time!"

On down the board I saw, "Make Money with Little Effort." Nothing to sell, nothing to buy. *Just get others* (emphasis mine) to try this new long distance company and make five percent profit off their long distance bills and their downline.

It's sad to see that large ministries and small are going this route to raise the necessary funds to operate.

The next one read, "Make Money Fast and Easy," and another said "Lazy Person's MLM." The text on that one read, "I love this money-making program because it does not take a lot of work but returns lots of profits quickly." It went on to say that profits are almost immediate and many are making at least $500 per day after 30-45 days. The ads lead you to believe that there's not much else to do but sit back on the sofa, grab the remote and start planning on ways to spend tons of money. Another ad read "Gold Coins! Secret Source." If you open the file, you'll see, "I can show you how to leverage a one-time deposit of $50 into $257,835 in gold coins and cash within a year."

The sad thing is that many in the Body of Christ are responding to all these unscriptural schemes, sucked in by the love of money. How can we be so blind?

Business as a Lifestyle

Laurie was motivated to build her business up to the point where her husband could quit his job. She had received wonderful results from the product and had her whole family taking it. Everything they did and everywhere they went revolved around the business. The whole family talked about the wonders of the product constantly. Every salesman who came to the door and every friend they invited over after church heard about it. They mentioned it at every social event they attended. Even out running errands they'd try to find some way to talk about the product and the business.

When unethical business practices and tainted products were uncovered, Laurie felt she could no longer represent the company. Since the whole family's life had revolved around the product, their lives changed greatly. Depression and bitterness set in.

When I was involved in building my business, relationships were only important if people were into "my thing" and had the potential to make me money. This is common in American business today. We are indoctrinated into believing that we should only hang around with people who are positive and supportive of us in our new ventures. We can get to the point where we tune out any and all opposition, including godly counsel. I actually began to believe that sharing my product and business was more important that sharing the Lord. I felt my way was the only way. It took the place of any kind of evangelism in my life! I went to church with business on my mind and encouraged thousands of others to do the same. I made friends with business on my mind and taught others to do the same.

When my friend, Bob, was still an unbeliever, one of his best friends, Jim, was a Christian whose parents were deeply involved in their home-based business. The only reason Bob knew Jim was a Christian was that he knew that he went to church regularly. Bob told me he could tell what Jim's parent's priorities were by the "get rich quick" books and tapes lying about and photos of yachts on their refrigerator. After Bob got saved, Jim expressed excitement about his salvation.

Bob's last real contact with Jim was after they both were married about eight years ago. Jim and his wife had invited Bob and Sue out to dinner at a nice restaurant. Bob and Sue had been praying for new Christian friends to fellowship with. They were hoping that renewing this relationship, separated by college and careers, might be the beginning of the Lord's answer to their prayers. The dinner turned out to be nothing more than a sales pitch. Jim's only interest in Bob and Sue was to get them signed up in their business. Jim expressed his disappointment, the two couples parted ways and they haven't seen each other since.

If Christ modeled relationship building as the key to ministry, it's a fair assumption that he expects the same from us. When the product or plan we are selling is more important than the relationship, the relationship is superficial at best and there is no opportunity for impact. It grieves me to realize that I know countless people who have had a similar experience with a friend. Many relationships have been destroyed by wrong heart motives.

When I was a guest on a Christian radio program recently, a caller shared the traumatic experience she had when she and her husband went to an evangelical church for some counseling. They had just been out of the military for a short time and were not sure which way to go for employment. This caused stress on the marriage and they needed some counseling to help them sort some things out. The volunteer counselors assigned to them suggested that their problems would be solved if they joined their particular multi-level organization. The caller said she felt crushed. She and her husband felt extremely vulnerable emotionally and were asking for help. Instead of help, all they found were those who wanted only to make a profit on them.

Mary shared with me that a woman turned to her in the prayer time of a service and said, "The Lord has a word for you." After the service the woman told her that God wanted her to start taking the product that she was selling. Mary added that she has been beckoned over to open car trunks after evening services to show her the "magic" product that would reduce her hips instantly or cause her to lose weight without diet or exercise. Mary and her husband had finally had enough when the pastors of the church called together a "few good men" and made a presentation about satellite dishes. Mary knew they would be descending onto the congregation soon afterwards. Mary and Jeff left that church in hopes of finding one with some integrity and righteousness.

In Donna's church, it was the leaders who used the people to get rich quick. The choir director, elders, pastor and assistant pastors would get the members whipped up about whatever was the hot fad at the moment. One young man who had just gotten saved drew all his savings out to buy a stock of water purifiers in accordance with what the pastor recommended. When he couldn't sell them, he had to take them all to a flea market and get pennies on the dollar just to get rid of them.

Hannah, who is in ministry full-time, recently brought me an audio tape she and her husband had received in the mail. It was a 60-minute testimonial of a well-known local pastor who had gone headlong into a network marketing program that sells magnet therapy to heal injuries in the body. The pastor convincingly told his story, mixing Scripture with marketing statements. He said, "I know one man who is making $60,000 a month without spending that much time working the business!" His tactic was to send the tape to people in the ministry who needed extra money to make ends meet, hoping to recruit them into his downline.

Dena and Jim have been missionaries in Guatemala for 25 years, translating the Bible into the Chorti language.

Home on furlough, they received word that one of their largest donors was unable to continue supporting them. This was a loss of over $1,000 a month. Quickly, a friend found a couple to make up that support for the remainder of their furlough. The new donors invited Dena and Jim to visit for the weekend. After an hour or so of small talk, the couple started to ask all sorts of questions about Dena's and Jim's hopes and plans for the future.

"Are you able to accomplish all that you have dreamed with your current financial situation?" The questions they asked hinted that God might not provide if they didn't help Him out a bit. "We have a way for you to fund your Bible translation so you'll never again want for support!"

Dena and Jim felt violated and set up. This couple had supported them for four months clearly with the motive of recruiting them into their business. When Dena and Jim turned them down, saying that any deviation from God's call on their lives could be disaster, the couple cut them off from any future support or encouragement.

I hear story after story of people in leadership getting involved in these programs. It is dangerous for those in ministry to use their credibility as ministers or missionaries to promote and earn a profit on other people. Many assume that because the pastor or elder or person in leadership is involved, it must be God! They don't bother to pray and ask God if it is right for them. The credibility of the leader or ministry is touted and held up to prove that the program has integrity and is God's will for the potential recruit.

I was trained by one of the best. The football coach turned insurance mogul taught us that to make it big you have to think "recruit, recruit, recruit."

"When you close your eyes," he'd say, "it's almost like you have the word 'potential recruit' tattooed on the inside of your eyelids! Every person you see is a prospect. Every one you see needs an extra $500-$1,000 a month!" We were spellbound. His motivational style held us in awe and challenged us to make a difference with our lives.

The truth is, in order to make it big in any of these programs, you must sell out. The only way to motivate others and make big money is to eat it, sleep it, and breathe it. You must be consumed by it. And the dream is the big money. Don't let anyone ever tell you differently. The only way I've ever seen people get that big money is to be consumed. You must filter out anything that gets in your way of success: people, marriage, family, ministry, activities, godly counsel, even the Holy Spirit's convicting power.

NINE

Selling the "Dream"

We used to hold "opportunity meetings" once a week. These were high-powered gatherings where designated leaders would present the business opportunity in a way that would work the people into a selling frenzy. The idea was to get them signed up that night and motivated to really "do it!" When things were really hot, we'd have meetings sometimes two and three times a week to capitalize on the momentum.

There are many books out there on how to be successful in network marketing. Chuck and I have even authored a few. The experts all teach that the best way to get people excited about the opportunity is to show them graphically how bad their current situation is. Then you offer to rescue them from the terrible financial trap they are in with your product or business opportunity.

To raise dissatisfaction with the status quo, you must knock down the credibility of corporate America, traditional small business, and franchises. If you can make these look as bad as possible, your solution will look good in contrast. While we were believers in the free enterprise system, we were convinced that a regular job where you have to punch a time clock and be submitted to a boss was the worst kind of life. It had no freedom, no independence, no joy, no future. In our presentations we'd raise fear that with an ordinary job, a person would never have enough money at the end of each month to get ahead. We reminded them of the important things in life: a big house, a nice car, private Christian schools, and nice vacations.

At one point, Chuck and I created a slide show for our opportunity meetings. It started out asking the question, "Whatever happened to the American Dream?" It went on to paint the following picture of discontent and frustration: "Back in the early 1900s only 10 percent of the population had to work for an employer. Since then, almost all of us have been sold on the idea that a steady job in a large company is the way to achieve our dreams. We call that the corporate dream, and it's a lie! It is a deception designed to benefit those organizations for which we work."

With rhythmic precision, the slide show went on to talk about the corporate ladder and how few positions there really are at the top. "If anyone is going to get those positions it will be a relative of the owner. What about all the politics you have to play to move up? The big corporations make you promises and then never keep them. You can't put your trust in them."

When insecurity about the future had been raised, we'd let them know that they could trust network marketing. It wasn't just a way. It was held up as the *only* way.

We'd ask, "Who dictates the kind of car you drive? The kind of home you live in? The kind of education you give your children? The amount you're able to give to the ministries or charities of your choice? The kind of vacations you take? Or how about retirement?"

The answer to those questions was designed to cause discontent and insecurity in the audience, "Your boss does by what he pays you!"

By this time, people would feel dissatisfied and angry about their bosses, their present jobs and their lack of financial freedom. Then we would zero in by asking questions like, "Are you keeping your head about debt level? Are you living from paycheck to paycheck? Is it *ever* going to get any better?" We'd raise the possibility of mergers, takeovers, cutbacks, layoffs, transfers, demotions and unfair evaluations. "Would a cold, calculated decision to eliminate your job be devastating to you?"

We really rubbed it in by suggesting that most people in the audience have handled all these problems by sending mom back to work. When the mom's away from the house eight to ten hours a day, the children no longer have the advantage of a full-time mom at home. She misses the experiences of helping the children develop, and by the time she does get home from work, she's tired and busy playing catch up.

"Once you calculate all the taxes, baby-sitters, second car payment and maintenance, lunches and additional wardrobe," we'd point out, "mom is only making about one dollar an hour to help pay the bills." Then, just before we made our case for network marketing, we would really throw some salt in the wounds. The next slide would read: "The sad fact is that the majority of Americans:

- Never establish an emergency savings fund,
- Never get out of debt,
- Can't afford to buy a house,
- Can't afford to start their own business,

- Can't afford to send their children to private school or college,
- Can't fund the ministries or charities of their choice,
- End up in poverty in their old age,
- And die never having enough money to make their dreams come true!"

The next slide confirmed with statistics that out of every 100 people at age 65:
- 54 percent have to live off others
- 36 percent are dead
- 5 percent are still working
- 4 percent are well off
- 1 percent are wealthy

And then the kicker: *"How are you doing so far?"*

By this time, every person in the room would be dissatisfied and discontented. Now don't get me wrong. I'm not saying that the statistics aren't true. I know there are many, many people who are unhappy with their current employment. But what if our job situation is just one of many ways the Lord purifies our motives and teaches us to be obedient and thankful in *all* circumstances? What if He is using our jobs to make us more like Him — meek and humble? In *Hearing God,* Peter Lord says:

> God is more interested in the development of your character than he is in changing your circumstances. God's committal to us centers around conformity to Christ. God is not interested in helping us develop a philosophy of escape from problems by more dependence on

Him. He wants us to have a philosophy of triumph in overcoming problems.

Therefore, you can expect that God's wisdom to you will deal more with the development of your character than with circumstances. He knows that when Christ is in charge in you, the circumstances will change you. He may or may not change the circumstance.

Are you asking God to give you a new job because of adverse conditions where you are at present? Often it is not his will to change your circumstances. He uses those circumstances to transform you![6]

I can no longer deny that the meetings and presentations we led were calculated to make you covet what someone else had and become discontent with what you have. We were not living by 1 Timothy 6:6 where it says, *"Godliness with contentment is great gain."*

Stacking the Odds in Our Favor

Our presentations didn't stop there. We would present the options you would have in business today. "How costly is it to start your own business? Buy a franchise? Become a doctor or lawyer?" Then we would show how the odds are stacked against an individual since 90 percent of all small businesses fail in the first five years. Next, we would examine the option of living off investment income, showing the discouraging fact that in order to generate $3,000 a month in interest, half a million dollars would need to be invested!

"Well, by now," we'd say, "it's obvious that there is only one way to make it, to survive, to be free, independent and successful. That is to get involved with our network marketing program! Why, the cost is minimal to get started. You could be part time and begin by sponsoring others and help them learn to sponsor others. You develop a network that pays you residual income for life."

To really make it stick, we'd ask people what they would spend all the extra money on that they would be making with our company. Pictures of new houses, private schools, boats and other recreational vehicles, safaris and cruises, and savings accounts would further entice involvement. I've even heard of some organizations where the men have their wives parade around in designer clothes and expensive jewelry to get the women excited.

The rest of the presentation was a smorgasbord of dreams and fantasies showing that, if you sponsor five people and they each sponsor five and they each do the same, pretty soon you have thousands upon thousands in your downline and you're making big bucks.

As I think back on how we would motivate people toward greed, the Scripture in Proverbs 15:2 burns in my heart, *"The tongue of the wise uses knowledge rightly, but the mouth of fools pours forth foolishness."*

What impressive presentations do not say is that a very small percentage of people who get involved in MLM ever make any substantial money. Fewer than 20 percent ever really make a profit in MLM. This means there are an awful lot of people losing money for every one who makes some!

Pushing the Right Buttons

We built our empire in an opportunity meeting format. It was chock full of testimonials about how great the products were, how the product saved a person's life, and how easy it was to make thousands without hardly any work at all. Recently, I got a letter in the mail with the same message as our slide show.

"Dear Fellow Entrepreneur,

Do you know what "residual income" is? I didn't until two-and-a-half years ago. At that time we were broke! My husband hurt his back and with a ninth grade education, it was hard for him to find a job. I was taught you had to go to school, get a job, slave for 30 years and hope for the best. In September of 1992, we began working a home-based business. I was extremely skeptical. Nonetheless, we worked hard, met a lot of people, had a lot of fun and made a lot of money.

Last Christmas, we went on a month-long vacation to the Caribbean. When we returned, there was a check in the mailbox for over $9000. That is residual income! Today, we live in a "street of dreams" home on 10 acres. We drive the cars of our choice. We have all the toys."

Two days before receiving that letter I got the following fax:

"Dear Friend:

We have recently discovered (by complete accident) what is the most incredible opportunity we have ever seen. We have made a lot of money in two tremendous businesses, but never, not ever have we seen a more powerful and quicker way to make an incredible sum of money. If you would like to make in excess of $10,000 in the next 2-4 weeks, please call me immediately. P.S. My associate and good friend made $116,000 his very first month! We're going to take this to the top and a lot of very good people are going along with us! Call me A.S.A.P.!"

Can you see the same buttons being pushed? Can you see how being committed to an employer and being content with the income that you have seems a stupid, narrow, weak attitude, that of a loser rather than a winner?

In my early years of involvement in financial services, the "coach" used to tell us that if we made $50-100,000 a year and produced a big organization with a lot of sales, we would be somebody — we'd be winners! If we weren't excited, motivated, making lots of contacts, sales, and money, we would be nobody — we'd be losers!

It now grieves my heart to see how these organizations and their inspirational leaders mold us into thinking that success in their program is the ultimate goal for which to live. Hebrews 13:5 says:

> *Let your conduct be without covetousness and be content with such things as you have. For He himself said I will never leave you or forsake you.*

For years I missed that Scripture in my Bible.

Fake It Till You Make It

I'll never forget my first experience in multi-level marketing. Everything was based on how much money we made. We didn't really have the cash to buy the trappings of success, but knew we could really do this business. So we went out and leased what we felt we needed to *look* successful and to attract some good people! The idea was, if they looked at you and wanted what you had, they'd likely join your team. They didn't exactly tell us that. But they did parade successful recruiters across the screen and up on the stage who had all these things. So, naturally, we assumed that in order to do what they were doing we needed to look like they did!

When Chuck and I moved up to Seattle from the Los Angeles area, I opened up a 3,500-square-foot office, leased expensive office equipment, huge plants, paintings and wall murals so we would look successful! I drove a red Merkur that went so fast I found it almost impossible to do the speed limit. Of course, I needed the toys: car phone, pager, and cell phone. We lived in a 4,000-square-foot English Tudor dream house. Everything we had was obtained "0 down," with the smallest payments we could get. This meant we financed what we wanted over four-, five- or six-year leases.

I must admit that the "coach" never encouraged us to go into debt. In fact, he preached "make money and save money." But the pressure to make it big and create a successful image toned down his admonitions to keep expenses low. I had learned as a young girl the way to get attention and recognition was to compete and win, so my deep fear of being rejected fueled a lot of these unhealthy business practices.

We were encouraged to build relationships with our recruits by having them over to our house and spending time "selling them the dream." Almost every night of the week we would have a different couple over for dinner. We would "wine them and dine them" asking thought provoking questions like, "What's your dream, Joe? What is it exactly that you want this business to do for you?"

As I look back on those days, I can't remember one time that we had friends, relatives or acquaintances over to our house for any other reason. All our activities were designed to build our business. We would have people over to our house in a prestigious section of Seattle and entertain them like royalty while the notice from the gas company threatening disconnection lay on my desk in the other room!

One evening we went out to dinner and a play with our newest "hot shot" recruit and his fiancé. They had been given free tickets to the play and we were going "dutch" for dinner. Chuck and I were so broke that we couldn't afford dinner. We had seven dollars to our name. We each ordered a salad, saying "Oh, we're really not hungry." I wonder now if they saw the yearning in our eyes as we watched them eat their New York steaks. Here I was making over $100,000 a year, but I was spending $150,000 just to keep the thing going!

I had a good friend who was really consumed by looking successful and creating the image of prosperity. She opened up a swank office in a suburb of Seattle with designer colors, high-end furnishings and the hottest office equipment available. Since Laurie was married to a doctor with a thriving practice, she was able to create a smoke screen of affluence by using his money and credit. For the entire time I knew her in business, she gave the appearance of being successful. In reality, she too was spending far more than she made just to keep up the front.

Mark was so intent on making it in the business that he would spend all his money advertising, taking people out to expensive restaurants, and generally acting like a "high roller." All the while Mark's wife, Marva, and their three children under the age of five were constantly stranded at home with no extra car, no money, no diapers and no food. All the family's money was being squandered on the business and looking successful — at the expense of the children's well-being!

In pretending to be something we are not and striving to get rich quick, we build our lives on shaky ground. A definition of pride is "wanting to be known for who you really aren't." Humility is "being willing to be known for who you really are."

Deceptive Practices

I learned from the "coach" that a great way to find prospects for the business was by going to events in the community, such as my children's little league games or anyplace there is a gathering. We were taught to get a conversation started with someone who looked like a good potential recruit. The more questions we asked about them, the more they would enjoy talking about themselves. But the trick we learned was to keep asking them about themselves, their jobs, their families, etc. Sooner or later, they would ask us, "What do you do for a living?" That would be what we were waiting for — the opening for us to recruit them into our business!

I also used and taught the technique of asking people "who do you know?" Let's face it. No one wants to be sold anything. So the best way to approach people is to ask them a question. I'd say something like this: "I know you're a busy person, and probably wouldn't even be interested, but who do you know who might be interested in making an extra $500 - $1,000 a month, part-time?"

Now, 50 percent of the time, the person is going to say, "Hey...what about me? I wouldn't mind earning that much extra money!" But if you had approached them with, "I'd like to show you a way to make some extra money" you would probably have scared them off.

Then the one that I fell for and taught others to use was asking for a person's opinion. If you let someone know that you value his opinion, he is going to be a lot easier to talk to and he will probably want to help you out. I'd teach others to go to the most aggressive, positive, successful people on your list and say this, "John, you know I really value your opinion and would like to ask for a favor. I'm thinking about getting involved in a new business and would like you to take a look at it and let me know what you think. I'd sure appreciate the input and it would help me evaluate the opportunity for myself." Of course, what you really want to do is get John onto your team; at the very least, he may refer others to you.

We really never wanted anyone's opinion unless it was positive. We weren't really interested in evaluating the business because we were already involved! We just knew that flattery worked. Asking for someone's opinion was an easy way to get someone to a meeting.

The most abused technique is to invite people over to your house for dinner and fellowship, only to have one of your "business associates" (or upline) conveniently drop by towards the end of the meal to help you recruit your guests. I was once convinced that these practices were O.K. I felt my business opportunity and products were so good, that whatever it took to get them an objective hearing was worth it. After all, I was doing them a favor by sharing it with them. They just didn't know it yet!

The Dangling Carrot

A friend of mine recently shared how his daughter and her husband had been recruited into a high-powered business after graduating from a Christian college. The parents wanted them to be successful and loaned the young couple thousands to help "build their business." They later learned the money was spent for an expensive car, $300 shoes and the like. The daughter convinced her folks that she was building on a firm foundation.

The company she was part of was dangling a pretty irresistible carrot. The top 24 people in the company would receive lifetime income. If they worked hard for the next two or three years, they would be set for life! It wasn't long before the young couple had racked up over $100,000 in bills flying all over the country "building their business." Today they are divorced and have filed for bankruptcy.

Part of "selling the dream" would be getting people to make emotional decisions to get involved.

"If you don't get started now, just think of all the people you know that someone else might recruit! Why just last week we had a guy in the meeting who came with someone he had just met at church. He was so excited about this opportunity he signed up on the spot! His sister had been at a meeting the week before and was still trying to decide whether to do the business or not! Boy, was she regretting that she didn't sign up and get to him first!"

We certainly never suggested that anyone pray and ask the Lord if this was something he or she was supposed to be involved with. We never admitted that, while the program might be O.K. for one person, it may not be for another. The frenzy to build, build, build, and block out all negatives, kept us channeling our energies into signing everyone up in our program with whom we came in contact.

In all sales programs you're taught to "get 'em while they're hot!" God's will never seems to come up as a consideration! I now regret every time I got someone to do the business because I talked them into it. I can't remember an instance when anyone took time to find out if it was God's will for his life. I was so convinced that what I was doing was right, and so consumed by becoming successful, that I never even considered that my way wasn't necessarily right for everyone. My motto was, "Do it now! Get on this team, 'cuz we're going somewhere. They say opportunity only knocks twice. Is this your first chance, or your last?"

What presumption and pride! Proverbs 19:1-2 says,

> *Better is a poor man who walks in his integrity than he who is perverse in speech and is a fool. Also, it is not good for a person to be without knowledge, and he who makes haste with his feet errs.*

The Living Bible reads,

Better be poor and honest than rich and dishonest. It is dangerous and sinful to rush into the unknown.

Today, I get at least five calls a week from fellow believers trying to recruit us into a new program.

"Hey Athena, I was just thinking about you the other day. I know how successful you've been in the past and I just checked out the most awesome new company that you just have to take a look at! They're in their first year with over five million in sales and are completely debt free. My upline made over $40,000 last month already!"

I know from experience that these people are just doing what they've been trained to do: to push all the right buttons, and if possible, get the expert upline on the phone with their prospect so they can catch that "big fish." That, by the way, is one of the big dreams — to recruit someone who is a "heavy hitter" with a large following. If you can get someone like that involved, you can kick back, put your feet up, and watch the checks roll in.

When I get those calls almost every day, I practically feel like an ex-hooker. "Hi Athena, can I use you for a while so that I can get what I want?"

How can we as Christians ignore the words of Proverbs 28:19-20,

He who tills his land will have plenty of bread, but he who follows frivolity will have poverty enough! A faithful man will abound with blessings, but he who hastens to be rich will not go unpunished.

We sold the dream, and we sold it hard. We sold financial independence, lifetime residual income. We sold the things of the world and justified that if we had unlimited income that we could fund missions and ministries.

I have been greatly convicted by the words of Jesus in Luke 16:13-15,

> *'No servant can serve two masters; for either he will hate the one and love the other, or else he will be loyal to the one and despise the other. You cannot serve God and mammon.' Now the Pharisees, who were lovers of money, also heard all these things, and they derided Him. And He said to them, 'You are those who justify yourselves before men, but God knows your hearts. For what is highly esteemed among men is an abomination in the sight of God.'*

Making big money and becoming financially independent may be highly esteemed before men, but having our hearts consumed by that pursuit is an abomination in God's sight.

T E N

Miracle Workers
and
False Profits

Salespeople are an interesting bunch. We are so easily sold on an idea ourselves that, when we buy into a product or company, we go all out to get everyone we know excited about it. One company I represented had an herbal product that created the most amazing testimonials ever. At the meetings you would hear everything like deliverance from cigarettes, arthritis healed, blood pressure down to normal, asthma gone, and on and on. When a friend of mine went home and told her pastor husband about the meeting, he responded, "Hey, if you've got that product, who needs Jesus?"

You know, that really is a good question! With products that seemingly create life-changing results, we begin worshipping the product and its creator. Our zeal becomes directed towards getting people saved, well, or healed by the product we sell. The salesperson considers himself a miracle worker for the difference his product can make in lives.

Our focus is misdirected. What about Scriptures like James 5:13-15,

> *Is anyone among you suffering? Let him pray. Is anyone cheerful? Let him sing psalms. Is anyone among you sick? Let him call for the elders of the church, and let them pray over him, anointing him with oil in the name of the Lord. And the prayer of faith will save the sick, and the Lord will raise him up. And if he has committed sins, he will be forgiven.*

Why is it that we are always rushing to a "miracle cure" instead of rushing to the Master Physician?

Gimmicks in Disguise

In sales, you have to believe in what you are selling. Once you do, you seem to learn all the right buttons to push to get someone to buy your product. I would justify to myself that the product fills a need, so it's O.K. if I had to manipulate people to get them to buy it! I've found that many of the best sales training seminars around are based on the following techniques:

1) *Build rapport with the customer.*

The unsuspecting customers are warmed up by our friendly manner of complementing them on their house, their pets, whatever we can find to identify with. We mirror their body language. If they cross their legs, we cross our legs, if they fold their arms and sit back, we do the same. We spend a lot of time chitchatting, becoming "friends" to make them comfortable with us. We show them that we "care" about them. (If we really cared about them, we would be sharing the Lord with them.)

2) *Find out what your customer's hot buttons are.*

By finding out what is important to our customers, what their fears are, what makes them happy, what frustrates them, and what their goals and dreams are, we then have the ammunition we need to take the sales process into the direction we want.

3) *Gear our presentation to make our product or opportunity push our customer's hot buttons.*

We control the conversation. At the appropriate time, we throw into the sales presentation an explanation of how our product will give them what they want, relieve them of frustration, help them achieve their goal, or whatever. We are taught to "go for the close" when we push the hot button, and to use the assumptive close — why, they'd be crazy *not* to want to do this!

The Personality Test Gimmick

This technique reminds me of when I was involved in Scientology years before I became a Christian. I worked in the department that recruited new people into the organization and got them signed up for their first course. The gimmick the Church of Scientology used was a personality test. After the prospective client would take this test, it would be graded and all the areas where he graded low would be highlighted. These areas, we were trained to tell him, were ruining his life. Then, the close. We would always tell him that, no matter what the perceived problem area was, Scientology would help him handle it. There would always be deep emotions attached to the area of his life that was in shambles. The hope that Scientology could fix that problem would suck him right into spending hundreds and sometimes thousands of dollars just to "get better."

The sad part about this sales technique is that it works! It is one of the most successful forms of sales. Without being a high-pressure, arm-twisting kind of salesperson, you can subtly get your customer doing what you want him to do. These gimmicks are nothing less than manipulation and witchcraft.

A sales trainer I met told me story after story of how he would go through this three-step process and close the sale, or recruit the "big fish." One time he was selling a limited partnership opportunity to very wealthy businessmen on the East coast. He wined and dined one successful businessman, learning about all his weaknesses, frustrations, hopes and dreams over martinis in a dark corner of a prestigious hotel lounge. He then used all his ammunition to turn the meeting into a $100,000 commission for himself by painting a picture of stress-free living through income from the limited partnership. He pushed all his buttons and got what he wanted — his commission! This type of manipulation devalues people made in God's image. In fact, they almost become like a piece of meat or some other prize for the one who can successfully master the circumstance to their advantage.

My father used to tell me how he had a line that would always get him in the door when he was selling encyclopedias. He would get his foot inside the screen door, work magic with his words, and slide right into the house. He would push all the buttons he was trained to, silently insinuating that if the parents really loved their children, they would give them the gift of knowledge. He even recounted stories of single mothers on welfare to whom he would sell a $500 set of encyclopedias, all because he was such an incredible closer.

New Age Success Techniques

One major area of concern is the way "new age" success techniques have crept into most sales and multi-level organizations. Almost all consumer sales companies suggest that their representatives read *Think and Grow Rich* by Napolean Hill. Most use it for its helpful goal-setting techniques, but buried away in the last part of the book are rituals of calling up the wisdom of great men, like George Washington, who are dead. Calling up the wisdom of dead presidents sounds to me like some kind of séance.

Or how about *visualizing* the car we want, driving into the circular driveway in front of our 6,000-square-foot mansion, or our family vacationing on the beaches of Maui? Many leaders suggest that their people go to the Lexus or Mercedes new car lot and test drive their favorite model. As they drive around they are to *drink in the feel and sensation* of driving this luxury car. Afterwards, they are able to recreate in their minds that positive image of them driving their dream car. They are told their dreams will eventually become a reality. "If you can believe it, you can achieve it," is a favorite slogan in MLM.

One Christian leader I knew used to suggest that everyone close their eyes and see themselves standing in front of a room full of people with the idea that those people filling the room were all in their organization.

I've recently read the literature for a Christian MLM where you earn money by sponsoring a needy child. Only

25 percent of the money actually goes to the agency providing the support to these children. What disturbed me the most about this program was reading about their "Wealth Builders Series" and lending library. This is a program within their MLM where you can buy or borrow the "best books on success in the country." When I saw that they included books like *Think and Grow Rich* by Napolean Hill, I was really concerned.

Many Christians will now open the door to the enemy by using new age techniques to ensure their success in multi-level marketing! It's bad enough that this company is trying to link a worthwhile project like helping children with getting rich quick. They are trying to make it seem holy because the money being spent is going to a worthy cause. However, leading Christians into worldly and new age techniques is an outright abomination! Christians are being caught unaware in their drive to succeed.

There are even books that insinuate that Jesus was all in favor of multi-level marketing. One is named, *Jesus Was a Double-Diamond*. Yes, Jesus was a great example of networking. He told 12 who told some, who told some, who told some, and today we have millions and millions of Christians. I guess the glaring difference is that, in all the "telling" and "sharing," there was no financial reward involved. The heart motives were pure, even if man's pride and basic sin nature still got in the way. It does come down to heart motives, and when the bottom line is making money, you'd better watch out.

When salespeople consider themselves miracle workers, they are taking the glory away from God. Those who exploit others for their own selfish gain are making *false profits*. Where are the *prophets* in our day who will stand up for truth and righteousness?

SECTION III

"Go Forth and Make Money"

The Blinding Lights of Success

When the Lord convicted me and changed my heart, He also changed my definition of success. According to *The Concise Oxford Dictionary* there are three basic definitions for success:

The accomplishment of reaching a goal that was aimed at.

The attainment of wealth, fame or position.

Accomplishing one's purpose.

Success today means many things to many people. Without too much hesitation, I would have to say that "the accomplishment of reaching a goal that was aimed at" and "the attainment of wealth, fame or position" represent the world's point of view. "Accomplishing one's purpose" would be most appropriate for someone who calls himself a Christian.

How is purpose defined? In *Webster's Dictionary*, purpose is defined as "the object or end for which a thing is made."

For what were you made?

Was it to: get married, have a family, work at a job, build a business, earn over $50,000 a year, own a big house, buy a fast car, have an RV or a fishing boat in the driveway, have the kids in private school, vacation every year on the sandy beaches of Hawaii, and be financially independent?

Think about it for a minute. If that was our purpose in life, who would ever want to leave this earth? When I was deeply entrenched in my climb to the top, the last thing I wanted to do was die and go to heaven. Sitting around the throne and worshipping the Lord sounded boring when my eyes were on money and success.

Our purpose in life is to do the will of the Father. In fact, if Christ ascended into heaven and sent back His Holy Spirit to live in us, then we are the manifested Body of Christ on earth. The word manifest means to physically appear, so we are the physical body of Christ on earth. In 1 John 3:8b it reads, *"The Son of God appeared for this purpose, that He might destroy the works of the devil."* There you have the Christian's purpose as well...to destroy the works of the enemy. If every day of our Christian lives we make the choice to do the will of the Father and are obedient to His Word, we will surely destroy the works of the enemy.

But, it's hard to be obedient to what the Lord is telling you to do if you surround yourself with people who are consumed with the pursuit of worldly success and you are convinced that their business opportunity is for everyone else as well. The only way we can be a success as a Christian is to do what God is calling us to do. If we are obedient to what God's plan is for our lives, we will be a success in God's eyes. That may or may not include a hefty income or an annual vacation in Maui.

Sandra and Jim had spent two years striving for success in network marketing when they figured out that God was not calling them to that business. They no longer feel they have to spend every spare cent on "tools" such as books or tapes and major functions. They looked back on their experience and saw how easily they had been sucked in. They were told to, "Listen to a motivational tape a day, read fifteen minutes a day, go to all the meetings." All this activity was to motivate them to become a success which was measured only by the amount of money they made.

All the people who told them what great friends they would make in the business never call them anymore. Don and Sandy weren't able to keep the love of money out of their motivations for becoming involved in the business. They learned a hard life lesson in the process. Don wrote me recently saying, "I guess we'd rather be broke and in God's will than doing our own thing and rolling in the dough. God has always provided for us in the past and He has never let us down when we needed something. Life is short. Pray hard."

Because God created each of us to be unique individuals, He has a plan for each life He creates. If His plan for you is to be "salt and light" to other employees at a large corporation, anything else, including being a foreign missionary, is disobedience.

The only way for a Christian to experience true success is to have a deep, personal relationship with the living God — to hear His voice and to obey. If we are focused on worldly success, money, cars, a big house, vacations, and spending day in and day out listening to motivational tapes and thinking about succeeding in our business, it will be very, very difficult for us to have that deep walk that we are called to have with Jesus.

Whatever consumes our thoughts is what grows strong in our lives. In Matthew 6:19-21 Jesus said,

> *Do not lay up for yourselves treasures upon earth, where moth and rust destroy, and where thieves break in and steal. But lay up for yourselves treasures in heaven, where neither moth nor rust destroys, and where thieves do not break in or steal; for where your treasure is, there will your heart be also.*

I have a friend who, like me, came to know the Lord through the business in which she was involved. After hearing all the people testify about Jesus and how He helped them make $10, $20, $30 or $40,000 a month, Maren thought, *Maybe I should give this Jesus a try.* At a weekend-long regional rally, she attended the Sunday morning service where many of the top leaders in the organization shared their testimonies and a tremendous altar call closed the service. After her decision, she felt like she could really go full bore in the business because now God was on her side. Whenever she listened to a sermon or read the Word, she perked up over anything that seemed to encourage her in her business. At the same time, she turned a deaf ear to any Scripture that seemed to correct or convict her. All the while, her family was being neglected and her marriage was on the rocks. After years of being consumed with the pursuit of success in business, a near disaster brought Maren to her knees. She finally asked the Lord what He wanted her to do and it wasn't what she was doing.

Listen to the words of Job:

If I have put my confidence in gold, and called fine gold my trust, if I have gloated because my wealth was great, and because my hand had secured so much; if I have looked at the sun when it shone, or the moon going in splendor, and my heart became secretly enticed, and my hand threw a kiss from my mouth, that too would have been an iniquity calling for judgment, for I would have denied God above (Job 31:24-28).

Jeffrey has been tremendously successful in his business. His success came at a young age as he quickly rose to the top of his company. Earning in excess of a million dollars a year, Jeffrey has everything he could ever want including a mansion in the most expensive suburbs of Louisiana, complete with tennis and basketball courts, swimming pools and maids' quarters. He has a Mercedes, a Bentley, a yacht and a $500,000 RV. Jeffrey and Jennifer, his wife, have a condo in the south of France, other property in prime locations, a plush office and a personal library of antique books and artwork worth hundreds of thousands of dollars.

Their children have everything they could ever want and are educated at the best schools. The family travels the world and stays in five-star hotels. Jeffrey and Jennifer give incredible amounts to missions and their local church. They seem to live a fairy tale life.

But what has this success done to Jeffrey's spiritual life? Once an on-fire Christian, the last time I saw Jeffrey, he was seeing a psychologist twice a week, taking medication for depression and drinking an entire bottle of expensive wine every evening with dinner. He just couldn't seem to find happiness or peace. He had everything he could ever want — yet true fulfillment eluded him. I often wonder what Jeffrey would hear if he ever asked the Lord what He wanted to do with his life.

Have the blinding lights of success caused you to close your eyes to the Word of God? Has the glare caused you to just look the other way? Have you found yourself chasing after the world's definition of success? I know the pain you may be feeling right now. When God begins to convict us of our sin it can be, oh, so painful. But the joy of repenting before Him is worth the pain, just to have Him wash that sin away.

It may even be hard to imagine having the desire for God to really rule and reign in your life, letting go of the reins and allowing Him to have His way. I was always afraid that if I prayed, "Lord, Your will, not mine, use me, change me, mold me into the person You want me to be," He would make me give up all the things I loved in this life. Sometimes He does, sometimes He doesn't. But I can tell you, when you surrender to Him and make a quality decision to obey, *no matter what the consequences*, the joy and freedom you will experience will be better than the adrenaline rush of the world's success.

Body Count in the Church

The Church is fast becoming the casualty of an unseen war. In Vietnam, body count was the statistic used to determine if they were winning or losing the war. I see members of churches across America falling victim to the allurements of the world. We are being ambushed into thinking that we can spend the next five or ten years focusing on success so that we can spend the rest of our lives serving the Lord. If you think that doesn't sound like a bad thing, consider this from Peter Lord's *Hearing God:*

> "The now" — the precious present — is quite obviously the secret to a full life. How often we focus on the big events of the future — a family Christmas celebration, the coming conference, Father's Day, a high-school graduation. But God wants each of us, you and me, to focus on what is happening *today*, and the relevance of the Lord's voice regarding time is one of the ways to know the Shepherd's voice. His focus is always on "the now."

In contrast, the enemy tries to divert your attention to the past or the future. He knows that anyone who looks back on the pain of life will trip and stumble. *He also knows that a person who is concentrating on tomorrow is living in an illusion that prevents him from living fully now* (emphasis mine).[7]

The Vietnam War was not a conventional war, it was guerrilla warfare. When you're involved in a covert battle, you must understand how the enemy operates. In guerrilla warfare, soldiers choose a concealed position from which to fight. A picture postcard of an innocent, beautiful, lush green jungle may look like the perfect vacation spot, but if there is a war taking place you'll find something quite different. If you venture in, you will quickly find it full of booby traps and enemy soldiers wanting to do you harm or take you captive.

It is time for the Church to wake up. The body count of lifeless, unproductive (in the Kingdom), lukewarm Christians is rising at an alarming rate. I believe much of this crisis has to do with the scores of Christians who are striving for the love of money and the success of this world. As Christians, we *are* in a war...and it is a guerrilla war. The enemy does not come at you dressed in a red suit and carrying a pitchfork so you'll know who he is. He conceals his position and attacks us in subtle ways. Over time, if we're not watchful for the deceptive suggestions of the enemy, we may begin to act more like the world than we do the sanctified, set apart people we are chosen to be.

When the Lord first impressed upon me the need for this book, I was thinking that the problem was with man's wicked heart alone. As I prayed, God showed me that the elements at the core of the network marketing system are rotten. I don't feel Christians should be entangled with a system that is so opposed to the principles of His Word.

I am frequently asked, "Can you be a Christian and still be in MLM?" I would have to say, many Christians are. But my personal observation is, I have never yet met anyone in MLM who has been able to sustain a vibrant, totally dependent, flourishing relationship with God. I feel this is because of three things. First, because of the promotional hype at the core of multi-level that causes covetousness. Second, because the system fosters discontent. Third, because of the manipulation involved which causes blind following, rather than hearing God's voice and doing His will. With network marketing organizations built on worldly desires and entrenched with manipulation and greed, it would be hard to jump in the water without getting wet.

In *Experiencing God*, Blackaby and King compare and contrast God-centered living with self-centered living. They say,

> God-centered living is characterized by
> - confidence in God
> - dependence on God and His ability and provision
> - life focused on God and His activity
> - humbleness before God
> - denying self
> - seeking first the kingdom of God and His righteousness
> - seeking God's perspective in every circumstance
> - holy and godly living[8]

In contrast to God-centered living, self-centered living is characterized by
- life focused on self
- pride in self and self's accomplishments
- self-confidence
- depending on self and self's own abilities
- affirming self
- seeking to be acceptable to the world and its ways
- looking at circumstances from a human perspective
- selfish and ordinary living[9]

It is my opinion that MLM encourages self-centered, not God-centered living.

Covetousness, discontent and manipulation have also spread like poison through the Church. In living color on Christian television we've seen self-promotion at its worst, and blatant emotional manipulation to obtain money or a following. As long as we do not allow the Lord to deal with our worldly attitudes and heart motives, our fruit will be rotten.

A friend of mine who is an associate pastor was troubled when he heard I was writing this book. Frank and his wife, Flora, have tens of thousands of people in their sales organization selling a high-ticket personal-care line. They don't actively recruit people from church but their lifestyle of new cars, new homes, travel, vacations, and expensive clothes cannot help but be a lure.

Think about it; if you saw a couple living the "good life" and always talking about the vacation they just went on or the new house they just built, wouldn't you ask them what they did for a living? Wouldn't you be curious if a few Sundays out of every month the associate pastor was off traveling to some exotic place or holding a training convention in another city?

Frank tried to tell me that their company was different. He said that they don't focus on recruiting but on retailing; that they don't encourage people to recruit at church. When I reviewed the company video and training material, the familiar images of sandy beaches, big houses, and expensive cars flashed across the screen. The video called their business, "The opportunity of a lifetime with a stable, secure company; not your typical fly-by-night set up, but solid as a rock. Products that you can be proud of and an opportunity to make a significant income by building an organization."

Where is the focus? What are the buttons being pushed? What does this kind of recruiting material make us want in life? More of Jesus? I think not.

I believe the crux of the problem with most network marketing sales organizations is that, in order to build your business, you must use your contacts with friends, family and acquaintances. It's not selling something and making a profit that's wrong. But when you have to recruit everyone you know, using relationships for personal gain to be successful, it is almost impossible to keep pure heart motives.

A pastor writing me via e-mail agreed with my concerns about network marketing. But he assured me that he was a very balanced person and would not get consumed by the business. When I wrote him back, I posed some questions. What about the person in your congregation who finds out you are looking for people to help you in your business? What if that person gets completely consumed with the business and walks away from the Lord? Do you want that blood on your hands?

A main weakness of network marketing businesses is the requirement to build an organization in order to be successful. Most every company I know encourages you to build your organization with people who are "go-getter, type-A personalities." Something is wrong when you're trained to look for people who are workaholic, compulsive, and who have no boundaries because they'll go out there and make you money or make you look good.

Consider this when you recruit that mom who is trying to stay home with her kids and raise them to know and love God. When will she be spending time on the business? In many home-based businesses, the phone starts ringing at dinner time and usually doesn't quit until 9:00 P.M. or later. The business demands that she neglect her husband and children and serve her customers and the people in her organization. With so many of the people involved in network marketing being women, success goes right for the heart of the home — the mother.

Today in the church we have well-known pastors, missionaries, and even non-profit ministries getting involved in various money-making ventures. I know, I've recruited several myself. It's a shame that we don't take better care of those in the ministry by being faithful to tithe to the local church and give offerings to other ministries and missionaries who are doing the Lord's work. We have, by our own selfishness, forced many men and women of God to seek out other ways to make ends meet.

Phone and fax lines are humming as great opportunities are offered on a daily basis within the Body of Christ. Opportunity meetings are laced with Scripture verses and high-profile Christians are using their credibility in ministry to build their businesses. We have Christians — both leaders and lay people, spending all their time, resources, and energy chasing after great commissions instead of being involved in "The Great Commission."

Recently, I heard on the radio a man named John tell the story of going to a hype-filled opportunity meeting. When John asked about the necessity of focusing so much on money, the speaker announced that he was a Christian and quoted Ecclesiastes 10:19b *"Money is the answer to everything."* He insinuated that if John was in the Word more, he would know better than to ask such a foolish question. Christians are taking Scripture out of context to justify their actions, leading unsuspecting believers down a path of unrighteousness. We see Christians building large organizations of other Christians. They have big meetings where everyone is excited, up, positive and on-fire, not about Jesus and getting people saved, but about a business opportunity or miracle cure!

Satan never reveals the results of sin. The sin of adultery can look alluring on television dramas. You never see the destruction that it causes, the pain inflicted on the spouse, the devastation of the divorce, the heartbroken children. The enemy just lets you see the glitter. It appeals to your senses and leads you down the road of spiritual death.

The same thing happens in multi-level marketing. The enemy doesn't show you the divorces, bankruptcies, adultery, estranged children, destroyed friendships, and defeated Christians. He only shows you the big houses, the fancy cars, the vacations in Hawaii — the glitter.

The enemy will tempt you with that glitter when you're vulnerable. Remember when he tempted Jesus? He had been fasting for 40 days and His body was weak! That's when the enemy showed Him all that he would give Him if Jesus would just bow down and worship him. We must be aware of how the enemy tries the same thing in our lives.

Just think back to all the times you have been offered a "get rich quick" opportunity or some other possibility that appeals to the lust of the eyes or flesh. If you analyze it, you will probably see that you were at a vulnerable time in your life. Maybe you were out of money, or had just heard about layoffs coming. Whenever we are feeling a bit insecure about the future and fear sets in, watch out! Satan will be right there to tempt you!

Just a few weeks ago I received a letter in the mail. It looked like an ordinary chain letter — you know, the illegal kind! The cover letter was from a sweet sister in the Lord saying that she and her husband had been praying for a way to get the money to fix their roof. They felt that this "opportunity" was the way that the Lord was providing, saying that "He works in mysterious ways." The letter started out:

"Dear Friends:

Ordinarily I ignore chain letters and up to now I have never sent one out. But this one is different. It is only to women and it is only from friend to friend. We know who we are and each of us wants money for something worthwhile.

Jill Nelson says she ran this letter four times last year. The first time she received $10,000 and the other times nearly $7,000."

You are instructed to put a certain amount of money in a certain number of envelopes, to send them to the first four names on the list, adding your name and leaving off the top name. At the end of the letter these words appeared: "THIS IS NOT AN ILLEGAL LETTER."

Oh really? Says who? Who wrote this chain letter? Just because someone typed that statement on the bottom of the page, does that make it true? It made me wonder if the sister who had sent it out had really prayed about it.

Just out of curiosity, I called the attorney general's office to see if it was legal. Of course, it wasn't. Isn't it amazing that Christians would think that the Lord would provide money by illegal means!

Leaders Gone Astray

I very recently received an e-mail from Dan, a fellow believer. Dan shared his concern over the different programs going around in the church. He has a pastor friend in Alaska who is heavily promoting the grand-daddy of all network marketing organizations. When Dan saw him a few months ago for the first time in several years, he was amazed and grieved that the pastor only seemed to want to pitch the company, not to fellowship or talk about the Lord.

Don and Lori, who had been youth leaders years ago, had recently started attending a new church. Don quickly became an elder and Lori became involved in women's ministries. Within the last two years something has changed. Don resigned as an elder and Lori has all but given up the ministries in which she was involved. Their attendance at services has dropped to the point that their presence in one service every two months is the norm. Along with the drop in attendance and participation, they have been contacting members regularly to invite them to come to a business meeting. When they do come to church, they are usually accompanied by the same couple each time — their business associates. During times of fellowship, Don and Lori direct the couple to church members who have been selected for them to talk with. Anyone who is negative towards their pitch is told that they have "pre-conceived misconceptions" about the business because it is a "good Christian business opportunity." So far, every family they have gotten involved is now too busy attending weekend conventions to ever make it to church.

Another pastor who was once involved in several networking programs recently told me that the system does, in fact, do severe damage to the Body of Christ. He stated, "These companies suck the life-blood of the church away by taking up time, energy and resources. They misfocus the young, impressionable Christian and pervert holy relationships."

Paul tells me how his church is "crawling" with different programs. His concern is the pressure he feels to purchase out of guilt or love for other believers. Paul feels the main objective is not to sell, but to recruit. He said, "If the Lord has given us all such wonderful gifts of persuasion, let's use them to evangelize, not commercialize! Maybe I'm too bitter, but I am fed up with the constant invitations to 'parties' for overpriced products and skin care lines that don't do anything more than what I can find at the store!"

I could go on and on with the horror stories of Christians using "holy ground" to build their personal empires. We're so focused on making big money and all the things we can do with it, that we rarely hear the still, small voice of the Holy Spirit calling us to slow down, wait, be still and listen!

Hearing God

I cannot emphasize enough the importance of learning to hear God's voice. This is probably the one area in which most Christians are lacking. If we can learn to hear God's voice, we can be transformed into what the Lord really created us each to be. In *Hearing God*, Peter Lord lists the traps the enemy sets to keep us from hearing God's voice. They are:

The trap of hurry and busyness —
You can hear God better when you give Him quality time.

The trap of external distractions —
Filtering out external distractions will help you focus on what God wants to tell you.

The trap of not recognizing God's voice —
The more you get to know God, the more you recognize His voice.

The trap of our mind set —
You will be more sensitive to God's voice in all situations and among all people if you do not predetermine the most likely place to hear it.

The trap of trying too hard —
By recalling God's faithfulness in the past and his promises of guidance, we can learn to wait patiently for his answers.

The trap of presumption —
It is easy to shift from faith in God to faith in a
method or past experience.[10]

Pastor Lord cites the three major snares Satan uses as
roadblocks on our walk with Christ as:

The snare of rebellion —
The sin of rebellion is a decision to do what you
want, not what God wants.

The snare of double-mindedness —
A spiritually double-minded person is an individual who has not made up his mind to do God's
will, accept God's advice, or believe God's evaluation, no matter what it may be.

The snare of pretense —
Hypocritical is a word used to describe people
who are   pretentious. It manifests itself in many
ways — by Christians who pretend to be right
with God when they are not. They hope to impress others with their piety. But their pretense,
with a smile or a 'Praise the Lord' or 'I'm doing
fine,' goes both manward and Godward.[11]

We must be aware of the enemy's strategy if we are
going to successfully live the life He wants. And the only
way to live a life pleasing to Him is to hear His voice, and
obey.

Have We Been Robbed?

My attention has been drawn again and again to the book of Hosea. In the opening chapters the story is told of Hosea who is married to a prostitute named Gomer. When she goes astray, God keeps telling Hosea to take Gomer back. It is a beautiful message to us of God's heart towards His people. The rest of the book outlines the sinfulness of the nation Israel, God's punishment, His judgment and His mercy.

In Hosea 4:12, the Word says, *"For the spirit of harlotry has led them astray, and they have played the harlot, withdrawing themselves from subjection to their God."* Two of the definitions of harlotry are unfaithfulness and idolatry. Could it be that huge numbers of the body of Christ have been sucked into unfaithfulness and idolatry by committing their lives, energies, resources and affections to a business opportunity?

How are we led astray? By being consumed by a passion for more money, more recognition, more things.

How do we play the harlot?

I know when I got involved in network marketing, I was obsessed with thoughts about building an empire and a secure future, dreams for a bigger house, a nicer car, "the good life." I ran after the opportunity and spent all my resources on learning about it and getting good at it. It was the most important thing in my life. To me it *was* an idol.

How do we withdraw ourselves from subjection to God? We do what we want to do. We are inspired by other people to do something that seems right. We do what feels good and gives us a rush of adrenaline. We go 100 miles a minute and make decisions based on our common sense or that of the people training us, then we ask God to bless it. Willful and repeated sin gives the enemy legal rights to us, and soon, we aren't even able to obey the Word of God.

The Fruits of Being Led Astray

How can we tell if we have been led astray by harlotry? The Scriptures are clear:

"Harlotry, wine, and new wine take away the heart, the mind, and spiritual understanding" (Hosea 4:11, Amp.). We will be heartless, unable to love like we once did, lacking compassion and sensitivity to the plight of others. There will be an empty hole where our heart used to be. We may not be able to think clearly, feeling absent minded and spaced out. Without spiritual understanding, we will have a hard time understanding God's Word. The deep things of God will escape us and we will not be growing in the Lord.

Joe was very successful in MLM, but he had definitely developed a hard heart toward anyone plagued with difficulties. He rationalized that those kind of people were just losers and he didn't need to waste his time with them.

"They shall eat and not have enough" (Hosea 4:10, Amp.). If our hearts are lured away by following success, we will never

150

be satisfied with what we have. No matter how much success we have it will never be enough.

Marvin was making over $50,000 a month and he still wasn't happy. He needed a bigger house, a faster car, more money in the bank, and always had to have a new goal to conquer. It didn't matter how much he had, it never was enough.

"They shall play the harlot and beget no increase" (Hosea 4:10 Amp.). If the spirit of harlotry has led us astray, we will "play the harlot" by giving our affections to other lovers (success) and away from our first love (Jesus). We will be lacking and wanting in different areas of our lives. We may have no increase spiritually, financially, in our marriage, or intellectually (all or some).

Milton and June were committed to their company. They knew it was the answer for their financial future. Although they were living on Milton's limited disability income, they changed every product in their home to their brand. At wholesale, many of the items were 25-50 percent more expensive than what they could buy at the store. They spent $200-300 on motivational tapes and books and never missed a rally. They could barely afford to put food on the table and clothe their children.

"My people habitually ask counsel of senseless wooden idols and their staff of wood instructs them, for the spirit of harlotry has led them astray" (Hosea 4:12 Amp.). In sales and marketing, the experts in the industry are the ones to which you listen. You ask counsel of those who are successful in the business. This, I believe, puts Christians in a very tenuous position. When Christians begin taking advice, counsel and

instruction from unbelievers, carnal Christians, or only those who are positive and supportive about their business and making a profit on them, they are in a position to be led astray.

John and Linda were committed. They were sold out. This was their ticket. One by one, they eliminated every friend who did not follow them into the business. They seldom went to church more than once or twice a month, as the company was now their church. For every decision they needed input on, they asked their upline or someone they looked up to in the organization. They became completely tunnel-visioned to the point that they even disassociated from family members who were not involved in the business.

Hosea 4:18 says, *"Their drink is rebellion."* When I was steeped in the pursuit of success, I found it very difficult to submit to authority. I did my thing, working 60-70 hours a week, neglecting my family and making major decisions without consulting my husband. I didn't want anyone to tell me what to do.

Hosea 5:4 (Amp.) says, *"Their doings will not permit them to return to their God, for the spirit of harlotry is within them, and they do not know God (they do not recognize, appreciate, give heed to or cherish the Lord)."* Those consumed by success begin to backslide and are unable to return or draw back to God, continuing to backslide. They do not know God's voice, because they have listened for too long to the voice of the world.

Tom was sure his opportunity was from God. He was so sure, he spent endless hours away from his family and church to make it a success. He found himself backsliding into unfaithful relationships over and over again. Yet those in his upline continued to enable him in his unhealthy behavior. He never listened to God's still, small voice, He just assumed that what the person on the stage was saying must be from God.

"They shall go with their flocks and herds to seek the Lord with all their possessions inquiring and requiring Him; but they will not find Him: He has withdrawn Himself from them" (Hosea 5:6 Amp.). I've seen people bounce from church to church and ministry to ministry, even moving their family and possessions to seek God, but never finding Him.

Nearly every Sunday, Brad would be at the altar. He never had any victory. He was consumed with making it in MLM, but never had success. He would tearfully petition the Lord at the altar to meet his needs, bless his business and give him prosperity. He never thought about what God wanted from him, only what he wanted from God.

Hosea 5:7 (NKJ) reads, *"They have dealt treacherously with the Lord, for they have begotten pagan children."* It is heartbreaking to see how many children of those consumed by their business have rejected the Lord, turned away, or are completely rebellious.

Until our daughter came back to the Lord and He began restoring our children, all of our children were prodigals — they were pagan children!

"My people are destroyed for lack of knowledge; because you (the priestly nation) have rejected knowledge, I will also reject you that you shall be no priest to Me; seeing you have forgotten the law of your

God, I will also forget your children. The more they increased and multiplied (in prosperity and power), the more they sinned against Me: I will change their glory into shame" (Hosea 4:6-7 Amp.). I see this Scripture as a warning to pastors and those in leadership and ministry. You are, whether you know it or not, leading many astray by your involvement in the pursuit of success. If we don't wake up, He will change our glory into shame!

A Call to the Church

If we truly begin to pray that God will teach us to love the things that He loves, hate the things that He hates, and spend quality time every day seeking His will (not our own), the church will be full of on-fire believers who are consumed with Him. If we sincerely ask the Lord to create a desire in us to hunger and thirst after righteousness (not success), and make a commitment to the Lord to *only* be involved in whatever His will is for our lives we will see radical change.

We need *God's ideas* not just good ideas. I believe when we draw a line and say, "I'm not moving ahead until I hear from You, Lord," we will be amazed at what will happen. If we could just get our agendas out of the way, submit to His will and His ways, and depend on Him to provide for our families, our ministries, our needs (not necessarily our wants), we would see God do creative miracles. I know. I've experienced it.

My prayer for the Body of Christ is that we would be sensitive to all the things we are doing that defile the Church; that we would be painfully aware of our true heart motives and ask the Lord to purify us. Only then will we be obedient enough to seek true revival in our own hearts, families, churches and communities.

Oswald Chambers said it so well in *My Utmost for His Highest:*

> *"And the very God of peace sanctify you wholly"* (1 Thess: 23-24).
>
> When we pray to be sanctified, are we prepared to face the standard of these verses? We take the term sanctification much too lightly. Are we prepared for what sanctification will cost? *It will cost an intense narrowing of all our interests on earth, and an immense broadening of all our interests in God.* Sanctification means intense concentration on God's point of view. It means every power of body, soul and spirit chained and kept for God's purpose only. Are we prepared for God to do in us all that He separated us for? And then after His work is done in us, are we prepared to separate ourselves to God even as Jesus did? *"For their sakes I sanctify Myself."* The reason some of us have not entered into the experience of sanctification is that we have not realized the meaning of sanctification from God's standpoint. Sanctification means being made one with Jesus so that the disposition that ruled Him will rule us. Are we prepared for what that will cost? *It will cost everything that is not of God in us...* (emphasis mine).[12]

We must get desperate for God to change us instead of running around trying to fix our financial condition and achieve success. The problem is not with the circumstances of our lives, the problem is us. If we don't let God deal with us and our desires, attitudes and heart motives, it won't matter how we much we change our surroundings.

Let's remember that we are in a war and the enemy loves to use success and the things of this world to pull us into a life of disobedience. If you're involved or thinking about delving into a high-income business opportunity, you must be on the alert. Proceed with extreme caution. It could be a matter of spiritual life and death — not only for you but also for those you influence.

Consider these thoughts from Oswald Chambers' *My Utmost for His Highest*:

> There are times when you cannot understand why you cannot do what you want to do. ***When God brings the blank space, see that you do not fill it in, but wait.*** The blank space may come in order to teach you what sanctification means or it may come after sanctification to teach you what service means. ***Never run before God's guidance. If there is the slightest doubt, then He is not guiding. Whenever there is doubt — don't*** (emphasis mine).[13]

Don't Just Do Something, Stand There!

A friend of mine once asked me, "Did you ever wonder why God decided to name us human *beings* rather than human *doings?*" I have always been a doing person, but God has changed me so I can wait for His guidance. I agree wholeheartedly with Blackaby and King's comments in *Experiencing God:*

Sometimes individuals and churches are so busy doing things they think will help God accomplish His purpose, that He can't get their attention long enough to use them as servants to accomplish what He wants. We often wear ourselves out and accomplish very little of value to the kingdom.

I think God is crying out and shouting to us, ***"Don't just do something. Stand there! Enter into a love relationship with Me. Get to know Me. Adjust your life to Me. Let Me love you and reveal Myself to you as I work through you"*** (emphasis mine).[14]

A New Life

When I first left my multi-level business, I went from $22,000 a month to practically nothing overnight. I've watched God strip away the impure motives and wrong thought processes and the world's way of thinking that had so consumed my way of life and looking at things. I have watched Him miraculously provide day by day, month by month. As we are faithful to tithe and only get involved in work that He had ordained for us, through diligent prayer and confirmation, believing Him even when it didn't make logical sense to us, God has blessed us. No, we are not rolling in dough. We have enough to pay the bills every month and have extra to give when a need arises. We are available to be involved in ministry when the Lord leads anytime, night or day. He is restoring our family. We have normal relationships with people at church. We have no hidden agendas for fellowshipping with anyone.

Oh, what freedom that is! What liberty it is to be available to minister to someone in the Body of Christ without any heart motives other than doing the Lord's will. The Lord truly has revolutionized my life and I am grateful that He has allowed me to share the process with you. I am not proud of my failures, my sin and my flesh, but I can tell you that He can deliver us from all our afflictions and set our feet on the rock!

While God is continuing to work in my life, walking out the lessons I've learned is not always easy. Although He is restoring our family, I still struggle with my relationships with my children. I still have the tendency to spend all my time working instead of cultivating and nurturing the relationships closest to me. I force myself to get up an hour before I have to wake Aaron up at 6:00 A.M. every morning so that I can get my heart settled before the Lord and spend quality time with Him that sets my day on an even keel. I am still inclined to focus my attention on things that are important to me, instead of concentrating on how I can minister to my husband and cherish our relationship.

But I am learning to live a balanced life, one that values relationship and God's will above all else. Our marriage is stronger today than it has ever been, as we walk through life as one-flesh, cherishing and nurturing one another and staying completely transparent before each other. Now I share Chuck's burning desire to see people saved and set free by the power of God. I have a strong desire to be sensitive to what the Lord is saying and doing, not only in my life but in the lives of others as well. I don't spend all my time scheming how I can do something that will prove my worth and importance. I am so full of His love, peace and acceptance that I don't need to seek recognition and strokes from others. He has truly transformed my life, and is continuing, as I yield myself, my rights, my hopes, my plans and my will to Him, to transfigure me day by day.

For years I was consumed with money, prestige and recognition. I ended up with broken relationships, a fractured family life, and spiritual drought. Now, I have chosen for the rest of my life to be consumed by the holy fire of God, consumed by His Spirit and consumed by His will. The result of that choice has been restored relationships with pure heart motives, a renewed family life full of depth and dimension, and a vital, energizing, zealous love-relationship with the Living God. There's no question in my mind that the choice I made was the right one.

A Call to Return to Our First Love

I pray that my experiences and how God has dealt with my heart will call some to return to their first love. In the book of the Revelation, Jesus says, *"Nevertheless I have this against you, that you have left your first love"* (Rev. 2:4). We have been running after other lovers for too long. Can you remember what it was like the first time you fell in love? As I pondered this, a flood of memories rushed in. I began to list the things I remembered about the way I acted.

Whenever I looked at him I would have to catch my breath.
I would wake up in the morning thinking about him and drift off to sleep at night doing the same.
His presence flooded my mind every waking minute of the day.
When I was with him I didn't want to leave.
When I was away from him I couldn't wait to see him again.
I was always thinking of new ways to fix myself up to please him.

I daydreamed about our future together.

I memorized every small detail of his face.

I would doodle his name on my notepad and then sign his last name after mine.

I had an intense desire to know everything about him.

I wanted all my friends to meet him.

He became way more important than my friends or other activities in my life.

We would spend hours on end sharing and just being together.

When I asked Chuck to think back on his first love, he shared from his perspective:

He changed his schedule so he could see her more often.

He did things he wouldn't ordinarily do.

He found out what she liked, the kind of clothes and cologne, and then set out to wear those things that pleased her.

He gave up going out with the boys to spend time with her.

He spent a whole lot of money on her.

He did silly things like buying her flowers, trinkets, and cards.

He wrote love poems and love letters...something he'd never done before.

As I looked over this list, my heart cried out in repentance to the Lord. "Oh God, forgive me for not loving you that way! Forgive me for not giving you my whole heart. ***Cause me to return to you and treat you in the same way I did my first love.*** For you alone are worthy of that kind of love. You alone are deserving of that kind of adoration." Help us Lord, as the Body of Christ, to return to our first love.

The words of the following song express my deep feelings about taking time with God. Yes, the important thing is the "heart of the matter."

THE HEART OF THE MATTER
Words and Music by Tim Pedigo (used by permission)

You wake up in the morning
Crawl out of bed
Gotta get moving but your
heartbeat says
Oh, take a little time out
You're in a hurry
Gotta make a little
more pay
Gotta keep the schedule
No time to pray
Oh, too busy rushin' about.

But the matter at hand
Is what's wrong with your heart
You lose the battle before you start
Then the holy flame dies out within
And your spiritual eyes
Grow sadly dim
You trust yourself
Instead of looking to Him
Oh my friend, that's the heart of
the matter.

CONSUMED BY SUCCESS

You're hardly out the door
When you encounter the foe
Walls start fallin' like dominoes
Oh, but there's still a way out
Though you're caught up
in the rubble
Of a man-made plan
And you realize things are
out of hand
Oh, you've gotta take time out.

But the matter at hand
Is what's wrong with your heart
You lose the battle before you start
Then the holy flame dies out within
And your spiritual eyes
Grow sadly dim
You trust yourself
Instead of looking to Him
Oh my friend, that's the heart of
the matter.

Your head hits the pillow
As the day draws in
Battered, defeated, and
alone again
Oh, a little voice cries out
Oh, take a little time out
Oh, take a little time out.

SECTION IV

"Setting the Captives Free"

FOURTEEN

You Can Be Free From the Trap

One sign of an emotionally healthy person is that he or she is open to new information and open to other opinions. It is very dangerous to be so closed-minded that you never receive other viewpoints or input. In fact, that is how many people find themselves involved in cults.

When I was involved in Scientology, I was convinced that it was right for everyone. I was not open to differing opinions. When I noticed things that weren't quite right I'd ignore them, because way down deep I knew I would lose my friends and support system if I ever doubted the organization. While I didn't realize it at the time, fear kept me involved. I didn't allow myself to hear any ideas that opposed my beliefs because it might rock the boat. I was afraid to lose my identity. In *The Kingdom of the Cults*, Walter Martin states, "First and foremost, the belief systems of the cults are characterized by closed-mindedness. They are not interested in rational cognitive evaluation of the facts."[15]

It is just as easy to be convinced about a business opportunity to the point of unhealthy closed-mindedness. Especially if you've built your world around your opportunity. Breaking free from the trap may seem like a scary thought, but please, be open, and see what the Lord might be trying to say to your heart.

Are you, or is someone you love, trapped in the web of success? If you're still not sure, take the Heart Check-up. Answer the questions as honestly as you can. (If you have a loved one you're concerned about, answer the questions about them from your perspective.)

Heart Check-up

	YES	NO
Do you spend more time each day thinking about how to build your business than you do the Lord?		
Do you view people in general (friends, family and acquaintances) as a means to an end (i.e. your success in business)?		
Do you consider the negative comments about your product or opportunity as an evil scheme from the devil to steal your dream?		
Do you believe your opportunity to be the best way for anyone who wants to earn extra money to fulfill that desire?		
Do you find yourself talking more about your product/opportunity than you do the things of God?		
Are you more excited, animated, talkative and enthusiastic about your opportunity than you are about talking to a friend about Jesus?		

	YES	NO
Do you find yourself fellowshipping exclusively with those who are involved and/or positive about your business?		
Are you frustrated, angry and even a little bitter with your current employment situation? Do you see your "opportunity" as a way of escape from the bondage of your 9-5 job?		
Are you convinced that you owe it to your friends and family to share your opportunity with them?		
Do your business role models (those you aspire to be like) focus on big incomes, nice houses, new cars, annual vacations and financial independence?		
Do you tend to concentrate your time on relationships that help you build your business?		
Do you justify pouring your time, energy and resources into your business now because it will all pay off later?		

If you ended up with more than four or five yes answers, you, or your loved one, are trapped in the web of the unhealthy pursuit of success. But you can get free from the entanglement.

How to Break Free

Breaking free from the mindset of the unhealthy pursuit of success at any cost isn't always easy. The Lord needs to do a major overhaul on the values we hold and the way we view life. Most importantly, be open to the Lord, being willing to admit that you don't know what's best for your life, only Jesus does. It is only when we are completely yielded to the Lord that He can accomplish His perfect will in our lives. When He does that, we are a success! Start now by choosing to walk in these steps to freedom.

Steps to Freedom

1. Admit the possibility that you've made an error in judgment in getting involved in your current opportunity/career. *"There is a way that seems right to a man, but the end of which is death"* (Prov. 14:12).

2. Ask God to help you discern His voice above all the others. Commit yourself to learning to hear His voice and being obedient to what you hear. Read *Hearing God* by Peter Lord. *"The sheep hear His voice; and He calls His own sheep by name and leads them out"* (John 10:3b).

3. Ask God to show you your heart as He sees it. Be willing to see the bad as well as the good. *"Search me O God and know my heart, try me and see if there be any wicked way in me, and lead me in the way everlasting"* (Psalm 139:23-24).

4. Ask God to cause you to love the things that He loves and hate the things that He hates. Pray that He would break

you, change you, purify you, cleanse you. *"Create in me a clean heart O God, and renew a right spirit within me"* (Psalm 51:10).

5. Allow the Lord to convict your heart, especially in the areas of relationships and your heart motives, and the idolatry of being consumed by success instead of Jesus. Write down everything He shows you. *"The heart is deceitful above all things, and desperately wicked; who can know it? I the Lord, search the heart, I test the mind, even to give every man according to his ways, and according to the fruit of his doings"* (Jeremiah 17:9-10).

6. Confess to the Lord the sins you have written down. Repent (which means turn away from) and ask Him to forgive you. *"If we confess our sins He is faithful and just to forgive us our sins and cleanse us from all unrighteousness"* (I John 1:9).

7. Ask the Lord if there are unresolved issues in your life that have driven you to find comfort in your business. If He shows you some areas of wounding or abuse, ask Him to begin to heal your heart and He will tenderly do so. If more help is needed, seek out Bible-based Christian counseling or a support group to help you work through your issues. *"He heals the brokenhearted and binds up their wounds"* (Psalm 147:3).

8. Pray for discernment and godly wisdom. Also, take authority in the name of Jesus over double-mindedness. *"If any of you lacks wisdom, let him ask of God, who gives to all liberally and without reproach, and it will be given to him. But let him ask in faith, with no doubting, for he who doubts is like a wave of the sea driven and tossed by the wind. For let not that man suppose that he*

will receive anything from the Lord; he is a double-minded man, unstable in all his ways" (James 1:5-8).

9. Make a conscious effort to surround yourself with people who are hungry for more of God. Meet regularly with other Christians. Ask God to send you a prayer partner. Start learning about establishing healthy boundaries in relationships, work, and life in general. *"The righteous should choose his friends carefully, for the way of the wicked leads them astray"* (Prov. 12:26).

10. Surrender yourself completely to Jesus. Pray, "Have Your way, Lord!" Set aside all personal agendas and tell the Lord that you want His perfect will for your life. Read *Experiencing God — How to Live the Full Adventure of Knowing and Doing the Will of God* by Henry T. Blackaby & Claude V. King. *"Teach me to do Your will, for You are my God; Your Spirit is good. Lead me in the land of uprightness. Revive me, O Lord, for Your Name's sake! For Your righteousness' sake bring my soul out of trouble"* (Psalm 143:10-11).

11. Be willing to give it all up, to walk away, to die to your will, your plans, your agenda. *"Most assuredly, I say to you, unless a grain of wheat falls into the ground and dies, it remains alone; but if it dies, it produces much grain. He who loves his life will lose it, and he who hates his life in this world will keep it for eternal life. If anyone serves Me, let him follow Me; and where I am, there My servant will be also. If anyone serves Me, him My Father will honor"* (John 12:24-26).

12. Ask God to show you what He wants for your life, how He wants to use your God-given gifts and talents. *"Commit your works to the Lord and your thoughts will be established"* (Prov. 16:3).

13. Be obedient, no matter how ridiculous it may seem. *"Let this mind be in you which was also in Christ Jesus, who, being in the form of God, did not consider it robbery to be equal with God, but made Himself of no reputation, taking the form of a servant, and coming in the likeness of men. And being found in appearance as a man, He humbled Himself and became obedient to the point of death, even the death of the cross"* (Philippians 2:5-8).

These steps may take weeks, months or even years, but the Lord will use each step of the way to soften your heart to His will and His ways. Be open to His guiding and confirmation as you walk through to freedom. Also, be careful not to get bitter towards those who have knowingly or unknowingly set traps (Psalm 140:5) for you in business. Many people who are inspiring others by using the ways of the world are not even aware they are doing so. Ask the Lord to help you have a forgiving heart. Then make a quality decision not to become offended at what others have done to you. Forgive them, for they know not what they do.

How to Repair Damaged Relationships

Now that you've seen the damage you've caused to the relationships in your life, it is important that you repair these relationships through repentance and asking forgiveness wherever possible. Here are a few steps to consider.

1. Prayerfully create a list of those you've harmed in building your business. Ask the Lord to bring names to your mind.

2. Write out exactly how you've hurt them.

171

For example: In my pursuit to be successful, I focused on using all my personal relationships to make money and "make it big." I called _____ on the phone and tried to rebuild our friendship with the hidden motive to recruit them into my business. This action devalued _____ as a person.

Or

In my enthusiasm to build my business, I used tactics that were not completely aboveboard. In fact, they were downright deceitful. In order to _____ I had to tell half-truths, and I got to the point where I believed the lies! Being dishonest in my communication with _____ defiled our relationship.

3. Wherever possible, go to the person you sinned against. Admit your wrong, confess your sin, repent and ask him or her to forgive you for misusing the relationship.

4. Make a personal commitment to the Lord to keep pure heart motives for all future relationships.

How to Help Others Break Free

The most important thing you can do to help others break free from the web of being consumed by success is pray. Pray that God would soften their hearts and cause them to be open to the truth. Your most powerful resource is prayer.

The Challenge

Are you at a crossroads where you are laying aside godly relationships to make money or using people to succeed? Are you attracted by easy money or motivated by financial success and all it has to offer?

I would say to you then, *"Choose you this day whom you will serve"* (Joshua 24:15).

Your choice will make a difference for eternity.

The Narrow Way

It's been six months now since the first printing of *Consumed by Success*. I've done scores of radio and TV interviews and no doubt made more than a few people angry. But over and over again, people call into these programs or write me later saying, "Yes! I always knew there was something wrong with multi-level marketing but I could never put my finger on it! You are the first person I've ever heard verbalize what I was feeling! Thank you!"

A pastor called in when I did the *Prime Time America* show on the Moody Network with Jim Warren. He shared how he had been involved in two different MLM programs and had almost missed his ministry calling. A woman called in when I was on the *Andy Anderson Live!* show and shared how her four-year-old daughter said to her, "Mommy, you love money more than you love me." It was then this mother knew she had to walk away from the whole thing. I've been confided in by some who have made it to the top in MLM and slowed down long enough to hear God's voice. They report, "what you are saying is oh so true!" Many have shared that God has spoken the same things to them and led them to repentance.

Majoring in the Minors

It has also been interesting to see how those still actively involved in MLM are reacting. So far, those who are "committed" to the success system of MLM and are actively building momentum don't seem to want to hear what I am saying. They have too much to protect, have blinders on and are unwilling to entertain the thought that God just might be speaking to them! Many of those I am upsetting with my message say things like, "Oh, she just had a bad experience. If she were with *my* company, she would feel differently about MLM," or "That was just Athena's problem. Only people who are workaholics like her would have a problem with MLM, so her message is not for me." They really don't want to hear the truth, so they major in the minors and miss the whole point.

My message has nothing to do with companies or products. There are good companies and bad companies, just as there are good products and bad products. My point is that we need to examine our heart motives and how the opportunity to make big money affects our spiritual lives. The problems I encountered in MLM do not relate only to those who tend to be Type-A personalities, it is just easier for people like me to get out of balance. The subtle mind-altering philosophies that encourage us to covet what others have and become discontent with what we have affects everyone involved in MLM.

On an hour-long radio program in Alabama almost all the callers agreed with what I was saying and shared their experiences of being solicited in church and feeling used and defiled. The host showed he was very much in favor of what I was saying, to the point of confronting one caller who tried to justify his involvement in MLM. Within 24 hours the largest distributor for the most well known MLM company in the country called the station and threatened to quit supporting the station if they didn't destroy the tape of our interview and get rid of the host. Within 30 days, the host was fired. It turns out that the entire radio station staff is steeped in various MLM programs to try to meet the station budget every month. They certainly didn't want to hear what I had to say!

Almost invariably someone will call in and tell how many people are being saved through their company and how, if it wasn't for their opportunity, they wouldn't have come to know the Lord. I can remember how we loved to use that rationale. I convinced myself that, because people in our business got saved at a company function, that made what I was doing "of God." That's typical for us sales types. We are always looking for an angle, for something we can use that will give us and our product or company credibility, something that will help us "sell" others on our idea. What the Lord has shown me is this. If He can use a donkey, He can surely use a company, or someone in that company, to get someone saved. That doesn't make the company great...it makes GOD great! He is the one who should be praised and glorified, not the company involved! 1 Corinthians 3:6 and 7 says: *"I planted, Apollos watered,* **but God gave the increase.** *So then neither he who plants is anything, nor he who waters,* **but God who gives the increase"** (emphasis mine).

When I recently saw the founder of a large MLM company on the cover of a well-known Christian magazine, I was deeply concerned. The interview painted a wonderful picture of this man and all the money he gives to ministries, (all of which I'm sure is true). Again, knowing the mind of a salesperson, every Christian involved in that company will be taking that magazine article and using it to prove that their opportunity is "of God."

I recently appeared on a national TV show. The couple who interviewed me mentioned their hesitation towards having me on since so many of their supporters are involved in MLM. Every time I would zero in on MLM, the host kept qualifying, "But that could be true about involvement in any kind of business."

As I pondered that statement, the Lord showed me the error in that thinking. Only MLM has the philosophy of recruiting a part-time army of distributors where anyone with a hundred dollars or so can get involved. This has the potential for a much more widespread effect on the Church, since just about everyone is a prospect. If someone were consumed by their real estate career or their climb up the corporate ladder (or their ministry for that matter) they still wouldn't be on the lookout for scores and scores of recruits with whom to build up their business. If someone were consumed with their law practice, they wouldn't necessarily be inspiring others to do the same and even helping them do so!

Many callers say, "I have my MLM business under control. I'm totally balanced and keep my priorities in order." I suggest that we all study 1 Corinthians 8:8 which says, *"...beware lest somehow this liberty of yours become a stumbling block to those who are weak."* If you are getting other people involved, you never know when a weaker brother or sister is going to be destroyed by the love of money and completely walk away from the Lord!

When I was on *Money Matters* with Larry Burkett, he shared the following:

"I have said many times, there's nothing fundamentally wrong with MLM — the difficulty is the motivation involved. What I have seen is that very few people are able to control that motivation, because more money breeds more money, and maybe more insidious than that, it breeds success — that feeling that I'm worth something to somebody other than my family and God. Receiving all that recognition and accolades can be a very dangerous thing.

"What Athena tells in a real way in her story is what I saw in a real way in an awful lot of the people I counseled back in the 70s and 80s. Typically, what I would see was one of the spouses — usually the more exuberant of the two — would get involved in an MLM program. They would then draw in the other spouse, because the company would encourage couples to "build the business" together. Immediately, it ended up drawing them both away from their family. Almost invariably, one of the two spouses, more often than not, the husband, would drop out, realizing he really didn't want to leave his job or change careers. The wife would stay involved, but now he would be taking care of the kids in the evenings while she attended motivational meetings and sales conferences. She would grow further and further estranged from him and would rationalize it by saying, 'We need the money...you're really not providing enough income for us to have the home or car we should have.' I saw many, many marriages destroyed — not because of MLM, but because they couldn't keep their motivation straight."[16]

His advice to his listeners regarding MLM was this:

"First: Know what God has called you to do and be sure you are doing that, whatever it is.

Second: Be a good steward first. Before you need any more money, you need to be a better steward of the money you already have. We have proved many times in the past with numerous couples that more money won't help their problem — infact, it only feeds the problem.

Third: If you're going to get involved, keep your recruiting efforts out of your church. I resigned my membership from a church once because the Sunday my wife and I stood up to join the church, three different people solicited me in the lobby for different MLM programs. I thought to myself, *boy, if the church leadership doesn't have that under control, they don't have anything under control!*

Fourth: If your bent in life is towards success and money and motivation, you need to flee these programs. They will destroy your life, they will destroy your family, and they will destroy your relationship with God."[17]

MLM has been coined "the wave of the future" by business experts. Yes, it is a good way for a company to get its product into the hands of the consumer. But is it good, *really good*, for those involved? I dare say, NO. I liken it to **contributing to the delinquency of a believer** if we bring someone into a situation where they are tempted and even encouraged to run after the things of the world. We must be ever diligent that the enemy will use even seemingly good things to distract us from God's true plan for our lives.

Can we continue, as Christians, to go down that wide road, the one that leads to destruction? Can we continue to flirt with the world to the extent that we fall into the category of those Jesus mentions in Revelation who *say* they are rich, but are really wretched, poor, blind, miserable and naked (see Rev.3:17)? No, we are called to take up our cross and follow Him. *The narrow way* calls us to say no to those things that would feed the lust of the flesh, the lust of the eyes and the pride of life. *The narrow way* calls us to live our lives without compromise, without justifying our sin away, without abusing the grace that is ours. *The narrow way* calls us to be quick to repent; to live in the light as He is in the light; to be so sensitive to the Holy Spirit that we would immediately know when we are out of line. *The narrow way* charges us to not just *say* we love Him, but to prove it by obeying all of His commands.

ENDNOTES

Chapter Seven

[1] Gothard, Bill. *Men's Manual, Volume II - Financial Freedom,* (Oak Brook, IL: Institute In Basic Youth Conflicts, 1983), pages 22-25.

[2] *Ibid.,* p. 23.

[3] *Ibid.,* p. 105.

[4] *Ibid.,* p. 105.

[5] *Ibid.,* p. 106-109.

Chapter Nine

[6] Lord, Peter. *Hearing God,* (Grand Rapids, MI: Baker, 1988), page 123.

Chapter Twelve

[7] Lord, Peter. *Hearing God,* (Grand Rapids, MI: Baker, 1988), pages 106, 107.

[8] Blackaby, King. *Experiencing God,* (Nashville, TN: Broadman & Holman, 1994), pages 63, 64.

[9] Blackaby, King. *Experiencing God,* (Nashville, TN: Broadman & Holman, 1994), page 64.

Chapter Thirteen

[10] Lord, Peter. *Hearing God,* (Grand Rapids, MI: Baker, 1988), pages 53-58.

[11] Lord, Peter. *Hearing God,* (Grand Rapids, MI: Baker, 1988), pages 65-70.

[12] Chambers, Oswald. *My Utmost for His Highest,* (Westwood, NJ: Barbour and Company, 1963), page 39.

[13] Chambers, Oswald. *My Utmost for His Highest,* (Westwood, NJ: Barbour and Company, 1963), page 4.

[14] Blackaby, King. *Experiencing God,* (Nashville, TN: Broadman & Holman, 1994), page 19.

Chapter Fourteen

[15] Martin, Walter. *The Kingdom of the Cults*, (Minneapolis, MN: Bethany House Publishers, 1985), page 26.

Epilogue

[16] Burkett, Larry. *Money Matters*, (Gainesville, GA: Christian Financial Concepts, 1996), live radio broadcast, April 23, 1996.

[17] Burkett, Larry. *Money Matters*, (Gainesville, GA: Christian Financial Concepts, 1996), live radio broadcast, April 23, 1996.

Suggested Reading

Blackaby, King. *Experiencing God.* Nashville, TN: Broadman & Holman, 1994.

Bridges, Jerry. *The Pursuit of Holiness.* Colorado Springs, CO: Navpress, 1978.

Cunningham, Loren. *Is That Really You, God?* Seattle, WA: YWAM Publishing, 1984.

Dawson, Joy. *Intimate Friendship with God.* Old Tappan, NJ: Chosen Books, 1986.

Dortch, Richard. *Fatal Conceit.* Green Forest, AR: New Leaf Press, 1993.

Gothard, Bill. *Men's Manual, Volume II - Financial Freedom.* Oak Brook, IL: Institute in Basic Youth Conflicts, 1983.

Hemflet, Minirth, Meier. *We Are Driven: The Compulsive Behaviors America Applauds.* Nashville, TN: Thomas Nelson Publishers, 1991.

Lord, Peter. *Hearing God.* Grand Rapids, MI: Baker, 1988.

Perkins, Bill. *Fatal Attractions: Overcoming Our Secret Addictions.* Eugene, OR: Harvest House Publishers, 1991.

Seamands, David. *Freedom from the Performance Trap.* Wheaton, IL: Victor Books, 1988.

Storey, Tim. *Good Idea or God Idea?* Orlando, FL: Creation House, 1994.

Wilkerson, David. *Hungry for More of Jesus.* Grand Rapids, MI: Chosen Books, 1992.

Commitment to Surrender

With God's help I will commit myself to live my life in honesty and truth, completely surrendered to His will and His ways.

- I will acknowledge my faults and ask forgivness.

- I will seek help when I need it.

- I will commit myself to learning to hear God's voice and then, by His grace, obey what I am hearing.

- I will return to my first love.

_____

Your signature

_____

Date

If you so desire, please make a copy of this form and send it to:

Athena Dean
The Narrow Way
PO Box 1406
Mukilteo, WA 98275
(206) 513-0769

Athena Dean's seminars, *"Issues of the Heart"* and
"Money, Motivation & The Master's Plan" are
available in workshop, retreat, or abbreviated
formats to meet the needs of the host organization.
For general or scheduling information,
please call (206) 513-0769.

To order additional copies of this book contact:

WinePress Publishing
PO Box 1406
Mukilteo, WA 98175

For quantity discount information
or to place an order by phone,
please call (800) 326-4674.

*All author royalties have been donated to non-profit ministries &
missionaries in the U.S. and Canada.*